What people are

AFTER HO

T0079820

Claire Millikin writes with deep feeling, craft, and delicacy about trauma; she makes obsessive, careful music — in the manner of Joseph Cornell's sublime work — from her repeated divinations of foreclosed and melancholy vistas. An astute critic as well as a scrupulous and admirably driven poet, she combines formal élan and emotional intensity. I think of her poems as following in the noble, painful tradition of Maurice Blanchot—language reaching toward silence.

— Wayne Koestenbaum
Distinguished Professor of English at the
City University of New York Graduate Center
author of *Blue Stranger With Mosaic Background* (2012)

As Claire Millikin puts it in the final poem of her *After Houses, Poetry for the Homeless,* "This is a book of escape & survival." Memory here does more than talk, it sings through eloquently detailed poems about exile from a beloved house, about "crossing thresholds" in cars with a baby, about growing older. Although all of us readers' lives differ, this book can also be shared as "our history. Don't turn away."

— Henry Braun, poet and peace activist
author of *Loyalty, New and Selected Poems* (2006)

Claire Millikin's deeply perceptive and elegiac poems remind us that the words we use to define the world are the same words that define our losses. Acknowledging the perilous journey of human survival, these poems teach us that "the four walls of/ a house may vanish if/ we do not define it." Both lush with language and haunting, *After Houses* is a work of uncanny beauty.

— Kathleen Ellis
author of *Vanishing Act* (2007)

The house, Gaston Bachelard tells us, "is our corner of the world . . . our first universe, a cosmos in every sense of the word." Millikin's hibernal, transient, gypsy economy of pawn and rent offers a hagiography not of sanctuary but of abandonment, vanishing, nightmare, salvage, banishment, and betrayal. In the triptych altars of dressing rooms, train station bathrooms, cinderblock restaurants, libraries, closets, cars, and the carapace of second-hand coats, the narrators of these haunted poems articulate an implacable, restive heimweh. "This history of tarnish and salvage wires my soul," says one speaker. That one never feels quite safe in these poems is testament to their post-Lapsarian truth and power.

— Lisa Russ Spear
author of *Vanitas, Rough: Poems* and
The Hide-and-Seek Muse: Annotations of Contemporary Poetry

AFTERHOUSES

AFTERHOUSES

Poetry for the Homeless by
Claire Millikin

Introduction by
Tara Betts

2LEAF PRESS

NEW YORK
www.2leafpress.org

P.O. Box 4378
Grand Central Station
New York, New York 10163-4378
editor@2leafpress.org
www.2leafpress.org

2LEAF PRESS
is an imprint of the
Intercultural Alliance of Artists & Scholars, Inc. (IAAS),
a NY-based nonprofit 501(c)(3) organization that promotes
multicultural literature and literacy.
www.theiaas.org

Cover photo: Gary Baller, Seattle's Union Gospel Mission, Copyright © 2007
Author Photo: Elisabeth Hogeman
Book design and layout: Gabrielle David

Library of Congress Control Number: 2014930044

ISBN-13: 978-1-940939-30-8 (Paperback)
ISBN-13: 978-1-940939-31-5 (eBook)

10   9   8   7   6   5   4   3   2   1

Published in the United States of America

First Edition | First Printing

The Publisher wishes to thank Seattle's Union Gospel Mission for the use of Gary Baller's photograph for *After Houses's* cover, and to Tara Betts for taking time from her busy schedule to write an introduction to this important poetry collection about homelessness.

2LEAF PRESS trade distribution is handled by University of Chicago Press / Chicago Distribution Center (www.press.uchicago.edu) 773.702.7010. Titles are also available for corporate, premium, and special sales. Please direct inquiries to the UCP Sales Department, 773.702.7248.

for Donna Boguslav

Moi, je suis intact, et ca m'est égal

— Arthur Rimbaud

CONTENTS

BROKENDOORS

TRANSIENT SHELTERS

CLAIRE MILLIKIN

PREFACE

AFTER HOUSES was long in the making, even if in some ways its inception came about quickly. Some of the poems reflect a life, or lives, left behind; a few of its poems were written years and even decades ago. But of course no life is ever completely shed as we move from skin to skin, and some of the poems contending with more difficult topics, I think, could never have been written had I not landed in a situation of relative stability, teaching as a Lecturer at the University of Virginia. Back when I was an intermittent student in New York City, Galway Kinnell told me not to try to publish too soon; he thought I was too fragile for it. And that strange advice, strangely, was good. The poems in *After Houses* then were written without the thought or intention of other people reading them. I think I've gotten so deeply into that habit of using the space of the poem as a place of intense privacy, even though now some of my poems have been published, I would never begin a poem with the thought that someone else might read it, with the concern for another's taste.

Why and how this book came to be a book about homelessness and longing for home is a complicated question. Uncomfortable as I am with the direct confessional mode, it is still important to say that for some years, and in my heart even now, I lived on the edge or with the near-threat of homelessness. Not because I was born into poverty, but for other reasons, reasons that I would have to sum up as my propensity for nightmares, a feeling that nowhere is safe, no person can be trusted; and so one keeps moving until suddenly one is living in one's inherited car. But over time as things stabilized for me, I grew obsessed with the metaphysics of homelessness, obsessed with the ways that homelessness marks America, with the ways that homelessness like poverty is often, of course not always, a female problem. As I grew older and became a less troubled person myself, I got haunted by other daughters — not in an activist way, but as I say metaphysically. What does homelessness mean for the soul? What does it mean to be a tenant, angling to meet the terms of retaining a roof and walls? Can we understand systems of capitalism and heteronormativity through the lens of homelessness? These are strange questions to address in poetry, and I do not address them through analysis. Instead they are part of the nightmare or haunting that is still with me even as, to be very clear, I now live in a house that my spouse and I own.

I think of Walter Benjamin's evocative and profound claim that all that is written should be written for the memory of God. I've probably muddled the way Benjamin put that, but the idea of writing for the memory of some force that sees through surfaces is what I try to do. Seeing through — I have a recurrent dream of going to my uncle's farm, or sometimes the farm of my childhood best friend (neither of these places exist anymore), and digging in the earth because words are there that need to be translated. It is not really a pleasant dream. But the act of translation is the transformative act of poetry, or the kind of poetry I try to write. When I first started writing poetry, the main thing I read was the dictionary. Each word, its etymology, seemed a poem, a series of histories and images embedded in the word.

To move from the earth, that is history or the body's history, to something else — words that carry images — is the goal of the poem, as I understand the act. I did not intend *After Houses* to be poems that document trauma. I reserve the space of the poem as a place that is completely its own, without any truth but its own parameters and perimeter. It is not a court of law, a confession, or a political edifice, at least not in my intention. That said, the poems were written with every effort to follow a line that might turn into a kind of transmutation, an alchemy. We are no longer in an historical era that cares so much about words, that is, we do not believe that words are magic, that they make the world. But I do believe the world is made of the words through which we speak and see.

CLAIRE MILLIKIN

I have written these poems more or less on-the-fly, in the specific sense that no one has paid me money to have a sequestered time for writing these poems. But I have needed that time and forced the matter, I guess. In the years during which the poems were written I developed a kind of ritual of small disappearances from other responsibilities (external necessities, always shifting). Given any gap of time, I sit at the desk and find the thing that needs to be said, that wants to be said. I guess the addiction to that moment of clarity that only a poem can yield is the force that drives the engine. For the world does not make sense without poems, and each poem shapes a world in which things can be clearly seen. That clarity is what I've longed for, and sought in poems about the unseen sacrifices and scars of daughters who do not survive, or who barely make it. I hope *After Houses* is a book that inspires some daughters to persevere, in whatever mode or manner that may be for her. ❖

— Claire Millikin
January, 2014

INTRODUCTION

I KEPT TURNING OVER the idea of homelessness. I was trying to find words for these poems that chilled me and kept working toward noticing the minutiae of all the small shelters that people take for granted in these two sections of poems under the headings "Broken Doors" and "Transient Shelters." After all, what is left "after houses"?

When Millikin says "My house is a story burned down," this line kept haunting me. Readers have to wonder what existed before the cinders and what the ashes might be hiding. The speaker's imagination is the one interior space that remains intact even as the possibilities for a roof remain impermanent. Readers see birds flapping their wings and escaping from a German romantic poet's pages. There are recollections of the last apartment where death resides and the one remaining photograph that is finally lost.

The recurrent images become confessions of sorts, where the secrets about survival and shame are laid bare. When *After Houses*, shows how a girl finds shelter in pawning rings, clothing store dressing rooms, abandoned houses, rented rooms, a train station bathroom, coats and thrift store clothes, cars and buses, even libraries serve as an escape.

Millikin complicates this idea of shelter by taking readers into the architectural and historical terms for types of roofs ring with the ancient need for shelter—architrave, narthex, stele. Even the ability and privilege to lock and close a door that is prized, and this is no echo of Virginia Woolf's *A Room of One's Own*. It is more immediate to our economic times and the urgent needs of women and girls who try to find a place to sleep and stay warm, even if it means trading their bodies and foraging and cultivating makeshift gardens that grow in the wild. The cultivated rows of a home are absent. She is even hyper-conscious of her status when finally entering another house when she places her shoes at the door.

When the voice of a young girl inhabits this earlier half of the book, it puts me in the mind of what Jeannette Walls chronicles with her own parents in the memoir *The Glass Castle,* except this is what happens when the girl does not have a reprieve from being homeless, and the lack of comfort and security that a home does not imply for her. That security bobs up in stark images that evoke the cold and fatality, such as in "Swimming Pools of Western Georgia":

> "The place that could drown you
> can always return, like evening that settles . . .
> Narrow shoulders exposed
> you rose from the water, refused a towel,
> the ropes of water sliding down
> like Houdini"

As *After Houses* progresses, it is evident how the working poor are never far from the cusp of homelessness either, when the speaker writes about being a waitress, or any other ways to find just enough. The hard, often thankless, and under recognized work that the country devalues and assigns to the working class and the poor and is often only partially documented in books like Barbara Ehrenreich's *Nickeled and Dimed* or the recent HBO documentary "Paycheck to Paycheck: The Life and Times of Katrina Gilbert." "Skirting Homelessness" directly addresses how personified homelessness can and does brutally circle those who try to establish a home.

Millikin makes these experiences multifaceted and reveals awareness rooted in survival. When the images of seeds, snow, and the idea of translation emerge, there is a seasonal shift, a time of growth, and the notion of finding a way to convey what a time after the last house was like, even if one comes back to doors that lock and close, which can even be alien and bitter like the salt, lead paint, leaded gas, mythically alchemical materials that repeat a motif of weariness and toxicity that even the rain cannot wash away.

As the book concludes, the closing of yet another cycle begins and makes itself seen. The speaker becomes a woman and a mother and signals a shift with poems like "The Grift Apartment" and "Fireflies" where the vulnerabilities incurred cause a deeper need: "The fireflies' thousand ulterior nerves/mark places where the world is too tender to touch, its desolate rented rooms."

Even the speaker's mother as a presence conjures up ideas of home, even as she is absent when this daughter becomes a mother. This idea "of elegy, of losing ground" in "Outer Banks" makes me wonder how Millikin makes us crave the anchor of steady ground again and again, even as it drops out like a hidden trap door beneath the feet of homeless people every day. In "Transatlantic Flights," that fear is always holding, just as firm as a plane steady in flight: "... How it tightens later, // gravity's hold, flex / that catches all and lets it fall."

Millikin's *After Houses* holds her readers steadfast through the world of homelessness without flinching. She reveals the gendered and classed complexities that make these poems a presence where there should no longer be a void in the American narrative that has touted too many false dreams. ❖

— Tara Betts
March 31, 2014
Binghamton, NY

BROKENDOORS

The Ruins

When I was a child my father mistook me for his wife,
dressing me in a red shirt, cheap stuff.

Suitcase of salt and my hands on the latch,
from such lineage, he has vanished

and insects circle the hollows of the yard
their violent bodies expiate.

The smallest insects hit my eyes,
like the gaze of Odysseus down with the dead.

Back then, another man was the way out,
but I return alone now, tabescent

from the long fast,
where the house by tobacco fields waits, maculate

in the steps of retreating rain.
Kneel beneath a sky like spilled grass,

celandine. Chipped, damaged,
he has left me the house

and feral dogs mark the edges,
slipping through the western doorways.

On Wearing Pawned Rings

The grief they carry makes me dizzy, but I choose them anyway:
Onyx, Sapphire, Ruby, the semi-precious
given up by the desperate for the desperate.
Winter's almost over and grass dry and white and obsolete
of last year bends. Old gold rings
gleam on my fingers that have paid.

This history of tarnish and salvage wires my soul:
wearing pawned gold, there will be an easement at the end
of winter, an easing of the quick terms of loss.

If ever I found a ring's original owner
wouldn't the rooms of her abandoned house
open through the eyes and keys of her jewels —
leave the keys on the kitchen counter for the next tenant.
And the ring's nicked, its shimmering polish dented
like grass at the end of winter,
the same crushed places recur.

I take them to the jeweler to be cleaned and mended.
She understands.
Because rings from a pawn shop make the hand shine,
but at night when I lay them by the bedside
their former wearer must feel their possible return,
as if she and I could go back
and meet again at the restaurant of the happy Buddha,
our hands' jewels glinting in night air.

Beyond the tables, ocean shifts back and forth.
Marriage upon marriage, polluted harbor.
The face of the woman who pawns stays inscrutable,
as if she turned away in the act of love.

The Tin Can Virgin

They sanctified the restaurant where the Virgin once appeared,
in snow's thick, vestigial mirror:

polished the original back table, reliquary
food, koliva, more holy

than grain for the living. We ate in her honor,
and snow closed in catching us in the glass room:

two girls together in the Virgin's apartment.
We've almost thawed completely, but the wound persists

in secret, that knowledge of winter in the throat.
We lived by the frozen ocean

and snow coated the canned foods of our subsistence,
salvaged from the derelict church,

nougat of the Virgin, numen, nous, stationary on which to write
letters to the dead, for no one survives this taste.

The beauty of ice sears you
and you cannot return the same to the middle of the day.

Canned food of the Virgin, Sanctus,
lead solder illumination.

Clothing Store in the Town of Impossible Rebirth

Go there when there's nowhere next to live,
not homeless but renting rooms by the day,

tracking narrow back streets not to sell or buy,
only watch the tight cloth of light

stitch through branches and bricks and balked birds,
incandescent throats hemmed into voice. Go there:

an attic hidden above the town,
take the steps up to where the frayed women

mend garments. For nothing much,
I have bartered such coats of silk,

no one could touch me in iridescent plisse.
And I dream yet of cast-off skirts' cream vermilion,

collars of anlace, daggers, jaggery sugar thirst.
To enter the kingdom of heaven as a child,

kneel at the door. Geniculate,
haunted by nakedness,

the women stitched across my shoulders
their hands shaking

cigarette's less opulent glitter, women
who asked nothing but touch as payment.

To sell yourself, a small pinch when the needle
pricks the weft of flesh and then rebirth.

In Dressing Rooms

Stumble across its lintel, some afternoons,
though it's no longer in business,
this store for gowns and ashes:
come to its gap with cigarettes cut
on the bias.

The seamstress
smokes her cigarettes on the corner of that long street,
and I do not forget her, I do not forget

how in the mirrors of her dressing rooms our bodies once glistened,
girls made of dark glass,
glim shimmer when the draw's past.

I knew the electric gaps of the walls were dangerous
and the power station gleaming on the corner fumed sulfur, and yet

in her dressing rooms we put away the world,
only our hands on buttons.

She pulled the threads
running the treadle with her distaff foot.

It wasn't anyone's fault
but I had to learn from someone how to dress,
with all the ribbons around my throat.

In That City By Water

Ducked into dressing rooms whenever I could,
to get out of the cold, snow falling through birds'
flights and voices, through human hands and doorways.

In dressing rooms you can outlast winter,
in love with the locked door,
trying on garment after garment,
to cover the stripped leaves of soul,
until the proprietor grows suspicious. Snow

falls like money past the windows.
I put on the knowledge
but could not pay for the merchandise, breath
by snow breath,
renting by my body each room
small enough for sky.

Only stay in the dressing room, stay.
Inside, no further harm can be done.

Button a coat not to buy,
closing across your throat the collar's harness:

next-door, the ocean carves its barriers closer and farther.
By a courtyard between buildings, snow-pearled trees.

Clothes of Snow

The house behind pines vanishes if I sway
slowly enough before it.

Only step farther in, and she will not yet
have sold the milk blue room
in which the mirrors stay awake
listening to grass against open doors,
in the small, fine feints of snow.

And she will not have sold the baby's bed
for its cold parameters,
face, hands, shoulders.

I am buying clothes of snow
to bring back
and dress before the mirror
however ephemeral, still intact.

The clothes of snow wear painfully,
it hurts to touch
like looking at your real face, the one you inherited.

But carefully keep the emptied drawers empty,
chifferobe spanning the gaps,
the faulted red shoes.

Snow slants into the room,
slowly unpack.

After Houses

There were no houses for us, only apartments,
then no apartments only streets,
then no streets, just water
moving in its coruscating channels toward dusk.

By doorways at night, fitful and intermittent,
I heard the ocean move
against its boundary, verge of salt,
arriving from the luminous places that cannot be sheltered.

We perched on the backs of someone else's inherited chairs,
chassis into night, and drank what was offered.
It must happen:
the ocean burns inward,
graphic inland levers of lost maps.
My house is a story burned down.

Working from hands in dreams,
pull from the abandoned garden
broken toys, stele, potsherds,
grandfather's arrowheads,
silenced Muskogee names.

After houses
along the flatlands
shake off the knowledge of blood,
raptors burying their shoulders into sky.

Library Cuirass

Borrowing her gray, frayed coat, walk
into the hiatal evening seeking kale, rhubarb,

and wheat, what the broken city yet grows
in secret furrows,

on roofs, and by abandoned train tracks.
For the way the body falls is always toward earth, sure

regressive turn,
slant of dusk. If I entered

this gate would lead
me like a soldier

down the hill to my former teacher who kneels
before her garden, her hands shaking,

pulling up the words, leaves, pages, fascicles, unbound
books for this last world.

Eschatology Apartment

We will buy at last the just apartment, justified against highway.
In gray cupboards, ambry of grisaille, we will store salt, apples, and rice.

Ocean marks the boundary of that city, and the highway that's stronger
than any other human world. We will purchase

an apartment where things end: highway, ocean.
Without bought furniture, the rooms swept hollow

like a bell through which traffic and tide echoes, timbre of light,
the counter some earlier tenants charred with cigarettes

we will polish until the harm's brilliant.
Somewhere beyond the highway, dark orchards persist.

For winter coats, we inherit our mothers'.
Nothing tastes of sorrow like a woman's hand-me-down,

so we'll cool our fevers by snow across the sills, at open windows,
through which we hear ceaselessly the western highway

bearing feldspar and karst, and sleep in shifts
to keep alert to the requiem light.

Lay down the terms of fallen leaves — oak, gingko, hickory.
No one else will want this place, abandoned, flush by the highway

inhabited by cries
of shorebirds, osprey, fulmar.

At the threshold: line up our shoes.
Once, we entered the world.

Dusk Boxes, Interiors

At evening the light from houses draws into the street
as if the houses were emptying, held in relief,

the way that paintings of seventeenth-century Dutch interiors
almost let you touch farther inward

but there is nothing at the center: a man at his table,
a woman sweeping a child's voice into silence.

I should not go out the way I do
into neighborhoods that don't know me

and trace the mercury bright orle around houses after supper, walking
where homelessness waits, at the boundary

a red lacquer chair set for mercy.
The houses empty into dusk's corridor

of nouns without verbs: too violent,
hunger on the skin trembles.

At dusk, the light in a house curves
a bell slightly wider than the house itself.

I will not be forgiven. Insects alighting
at summer's end cry, and other women call

their children back into doors, leaves swept
into the boxes of dusk.

When I was a child, mother's black hair grew long
enough to swim her hips.

Shadow Portrait

Only one true portrait
of me, and that is lost— thrown out with other detritus, behind a bridge, years
back.
We were waiting in the tent for sun to draw back,
darken down Ocracoke,

graveyard of the Atlantic, and my sister sketched me quick
in pencil scavenged from school, carried
in a rusted car on the ferry.

She traced, in profile, a face inherited,
sand slipping under our fingers
while I read about the ruins of Gibraltar—
damaged not lost.

Her eye and hand lost nothing, drew
onto torn paper a nine-year-old sister,
but the tent was not a house, and sky entered uneasily, taking all human things.

In those days before sunscreen we burned quickly,
bubbles rose on our skin, a poison
light sifting down, down, into the blood into the pulse,
light's abyss.

She never pursued art: father turned her hand.
There are times when light comes too close,
a bridge I should not want to cross, Goya's
shadows, tensed mathematics of dispersal.

Don't let it happen too fast, don't
Let it happen too fast.
There is only one portrait by which I'd know myself,
limned by my elder sister whose nakedness

when we first were women so terrified me that I trained
to run faster and faster until my heart beat into light like a boy's.

Hölderlin's Birds

I kept tracking the places in Hölderlin's poems
where he mentions birds:
each time I found a reference to birds the birds
flew from the pages and hid in my closet.
I locked the doors, but listened.

The birds cried violently, sometimes their cries sounded like engines
or like dinosaurs, atavistic pulse,
I remembered hearing from grandmother's kitchen,
by the windows
listening to what took place in the forest.

As in a bad dream, or a myth, it was my job to catch the places of birds
in Hölderlin's poems.
But the work carried such risk,
the birds flaring out against my hands, eyes, lips,
and no one believing afterwards
the source of blood.

I'd shield my face but it didn't always work,
the damage mounted. I persisted, not to be deterred
for I knew inside the words birds waited
and from inside the birds, souls emerged — violent and wild.
For the soul is a wound that takes flight
if you are reading Hölderlin.

The closets of my childhood filled with wings beating translation,
and my shoulders ached, fugitive —
to see at last for myself what he once saw
beneath the sun's killing weight
effulgerent fields, crossing
from another country back home
where no one was waiting, the beloved gone.

When We Could Not Be Innocent

We could not be innocent, in the beginning,
waiting tables with faces polished like children,

stashing in our pockets the nubile folded bills.
Rain stemmed the hickory branches,

smalto, mosaic that pulls apart, the tesserae
blue glass of fields, our hands open on the tables,

and the scent of fried meat in our hair like early sacrifice.
After a shift, I'd shower at his place to wash it out.

Careful not to be seen living in my sister's car,
gold light stroking the dashboard,

I accepted when he made his offer.
As down into the garden

of Eden the Lord once was drawn
by the smell of meat cooking at evening, a kind of homecoming

into the body: afternoon brings fevers and rain.

Frangi pani shaking begins again the terms of the garden,
where his natural daughter carries his sister's name.

The Falconer

I wanted to speak for myself.
But my eyes got seeled to train me to that voice.

Who knows whether he acted from love, desire, or need,
sewing my eyes shut. I fought to see between the threads:

a child can learn from her father's methods.
Uneasily the sky unfolds.

Pull out the threads, the garment
of light hurts for that new aperture.

To train a falcon needs heavy gloves, thickest leather.
For the bird will know your voice, homing to your cry,

devotion violent in its body, ever after.
Some grew accustomed to the seeled eyes,

clamped sight,
and would not look

after the stitches came out.
But when the fields burn back, and terraces dreams us,

falcons on the wheel, I cannot forget
his voice so late evening light

makes the room's walls look like marble, venous,
and all the birds come home.

Librarian of Salt

i.
No one much visited the special collections, and storms
came down frequently, a pattern like a scar.
How it hurt the first time
words suddenly opened. At the end
of the twelfth century, BC, Myceneans

began to vanish, their gold cups, lush burial sites
left behind in older weather.
Some hid by the coasts and some sought deeper, obscurer refuge.

From the golden cup of history, or childhood,
it's dangerous to drink.
The deer will turn suddenly
just before storm.

Renting a room by the library,
I climbed daily to the heavy doors.

ii.
At the end of childhood I returned to the library,
hiding from him, gathering new languages—mastering grammars,
golden cups of nouns—
my father never knew I had come back.
I set my hands, eyes, lips, to the task
of translation, a nerve
that heals only partly, lay-line by line.

Library for Tobacco

A place to get my hair cut under the table:
a farm house near pesticide spray, fields stilled in golden
dense molecules, his shoes
waiting at the door
as at the edge of water.

Books lined the walls
like stones in a chimney's interior.
He traced them with his fingers, patiently,
backward and forward through memory.

I had only to make one sacrifice
of myself, grant him the premise of domain,
the clock of the fields
that never entirely wound down.

Now, now the hour of the house
sways into itself, light steps down,
and the places he has squandered in my mouth
were surely worth the books. At last
one will do nearly anything
just to be allowed the time to read.

For his sisters' sons took him
back with their own. And I lay down
my shoes at the door and entered.

Cigarettes and the Infant

Against her nursery rules, he smoked.
Evenings, when the infant slept
windows widening with immanent vanishing sky,
propping open the eastern window he'd lean out
dragging on a cigarette,
swaying the smoke away from the crib
absently dropping ashes below.

He'd snuff the burning tip against his palm,
stigmata, the price he paid.
Smoking seemed to fit: the infant's
tender low breaths, each after the next,
inhale, exhale, audible life.
For the world can only begin again from ashes.

To hold the infant, he kept a coat in which he never smoked,
that the child might press its face against his chest
and not be touched by poisons of cigarette, cadmium, cyanide
pesticides of the Carolinas.

But when he'd kiss the small forehead
his lips impressed such memories of fire,
and the child builds its mind from a kiss.

Beyond the nursery stood winter,
and rain raked the dead grass.
The child's hands opened
reaching toward ocean,
to the left
behind the tall house.

CLAIRE MILLIKIN

The Lambs

In the deft and violent tenderness of spring
where to bring back the dead takes nothing but a voice
wind crossed the hill
bruising the light, leaf after leaf blew down,
a flinch of trees' backward shadows.

Mother slept late and we stepped to the school bus in darkness,
wrapping our coats tight to disguise our pelts, our nakedness,
stepping gingerly above glass fragments,
our hooves tender across bort.

We were not raised as human girls, for it cost our mother
too dearly to fend that turf,
our soft eyes and fur she tried to cover
and then gave up, exhausted.

She did not expect us to succeed,
neither in school nor marriage.
The house filled with angelic bells,
telephones left unanswered. For a cry,
for this lineage, the lamb.

The Snow Architect

He could build only with that one substance, snow: he knew the risks
the way his hands and mouth always tasted

like the burned place in a bad dream.
Ice caught his wrists as he shaped architrave, narthex.

But he would not leave the work,
for snow was his medium, it soothed him,

the small rooms of prostitution when it's too late
to turn and choose, his wife gone.

The snow set down mortal laws
impossible to interpret: white leaded paint

stalled by inertia in cabinets of slag,
as words in cold weather

come down to nouns, what must be said.
He could build only by risking this edge,

where the snow would fasten his mouth and knees and crotch.
The hardest part was getting right the sketch,

predicting the dimensions of the completed house
that room where you must sell yourself.

For the pencil of ice vanishes under hands' warm press,
a blue without depth, like objects dropped in dreams.

Dusk Waitress

At the end of childhood, I worked in a restaurant.
At dusk my father would enter, uninvited
and sit in my section on purpose, knowing I wanted nothing of it.

He would order a meal, gruffly, as if I had hurt him
his eyes on my apron front ties. Sweating
from the long shift,
I delivered, wordless, worldless, the food of furrowed dusk, succus.

Deer nosed the side of the restaurant, cinderblock.
I never asked another waitress to serve him

it never crossed my mind to protect myself,
or him, reflected in night's circumference
at the wide windows before the road out of town.
For bad dreams always lead to the same place.

Coin by coin, bring them to the register but don't count
yet the leaves shuttling for mercy,
shadows at the corner of sky
when he reaches into your pocket to pay.

Of Girls

A house by the falling river,
walls lined with photographs of former stars,
their names unrecognized, now, illegible, lipstick pressed kiss,
the house smelled of water, not unclean but dangerous,
water's depth pulling at the doors,
river carrying up the steps
atavistic silt.

We could not long for water when water already cornered us,
but thirst held in the faces of the beautiful,
vanished girls,
iridescent photographs,
this burden of wreckage and dilation

as in the shopping mall of childhood
when you purchase from Roses shoes and socks,
Roses, the store where your father once gave you a dollar
and said *spend it any way you want, girl.*

O rose of absolution,
the shop with a wound in its heart,
here is my photograph.

CLAIRE MILLIKIN

Train Station Bathroom at Night

The room sets almost holy, transfigured by winter's
ulterior scar. Outside, a freezing rain sinks.

You must wait until no footsteps sound
beyond the locked door. Holy, for here is a locked door,

and the room eternal, against
every gherao, every poem of force, nothing will enter

for these minutes. Immortal for nothing persists like space: innocent
to close the door against every man —

hands, eyes, the room inviolable as long as you run the water
door locked and the tap drawing leaden cold from a well.

No one should drink it, but you cannot stop
drawing its deft onyx stuff from beneath station bedrock.

All night trains will rock through by the double hours:
stay here sheltered, no one else speaks this language all yours

of stone floor and pocked walls and glassed leaves
in heaven's shadow.

The train station bathroom keeps everything suspended
as in dreams when you hear again your mother's voice.

A ticket in your pocket from a year ago,
for delectation comb your hair with fingers,

and in the mirror watch closely
this face echoing almost exactly your mother's face.

Train Station Bathroom Architecture

Greek Revival columns before dinted metal mirrors,
the rice of light spills downwards,
late at night when mostly the station empties
and birds pull down the highway
into vagrant rains. Gather

all useful that passengers have left behind.
Habitus, the rain's grisaille trespass:
for the passengers forsake their pens,
hairbrushes, telephones, golden rings. Once I wed
some unknown woman who had dropped her ring.

Cheap thing, I wore it like entering time,
at last a house of succor,
faux-diamond on my hand, culet,
rain veering inland along stairs towards tracks.
To make an account of myself:

my sister and I used to hide
where the yard slipped to gulley,
and we'd dig
deep into dirt, our fierce hands scraping it open.

Survival Sex

I am haunted
by transportation, pelagic rains
that cross above stations, startled birds crying in parsed light.

The buses bring daughters, fugitive
spilled-salt-girls along the walk;
beneath the wings of elms the buses cross.

Arrive again at the bus stations of childhood,
your teeth aching.
Recursive: an equation that calls and calls
back upon itself, the return of girls by buses,

for the violence of afternoon can be carried only by buses
climbing the desolate curve of roads between cities.

We arrive and vanish not into the world but into ourselves.

Sometimes, when I was small,
my parents held my hands as if they were made of pearl:
we walked by the lines of others' houses,
their shadows fierce as doves'.

Through windows the foyers of strangers glistened almost infinite,
a place without damage
for the bus has not stopped yet.

Anorexia Café

The wind almost blows it away for scant weight,
but, tenacious, the café holds fast.

In the anorexia café, everyone's welcome, though there's little food—
salt, mustard, a splurge of tomatoes grandfather grew
in the garden of his extremity, coterminous with clay fields.

The anorexia café shifts from country to country, carried
by raw open seeds, achene, indehiscent, in the palms of girls
who refused the pomegranate—wind blows the colder orchard,
pyrrhic light in dormer windows.

The anorexia café sets at storm's boundary: that hunger
that never eases, of heavy skies in late winter,
pine trees bending together.
For the girls wear diamond fragments on their brows.

And, really, there is no other language to learn but this ascesis.
Lanugo, soft fine hairs grow on their skin,
as they become children not women,
the café serving images only, imago mundi.

CLAIRE MILLIKIN

The Disappearance

Fog throws its setline,
the bay filling with opaque
rax, mist stretched so tight only the birds
can cross, immune to cars and language.

Just an afterimage, chorus, down the bones of a name.
Here is the world of objects,
an empty glass bottle casts,
in shadow shoulders, throat, and neck.

She'll be listed once in the newspapers and then it's done
a brief report of her birth and burial,
pale fallen apples, the orchard

abandoned a generation ago.

Hand in Glove

By the on-ramp to Interstate 75
in a persimmon tree, a pair of ruby gloves
among the ripening fruit,
the gloves' red more formal than blood.

The tree carried the gloves with such lightness,
as if it were nothing to be lost.

I too used to live hand to mouth,
by my wits,
swallowing nothing much but sugar and coffee, clothes
gathered in garbage bags in the back seat
of the car I'd inherited.

Scarlet, crimson, vermilion,
gloves that color aren't meant for warmth.

What I wouldn't refuse, out of hand;
money doesn't grow on trees.

Sharon fruit glisten on branches nacreous in frost.
Into the traffic
of my father's country
I merge, shaking.

CLAIRE MILLIKIN

Parking Lots of the
Nineteen-Seventies

Dry oak leaves on gravel, and a girl's lost shoe,
shadows tip beneath the trees

that frame the late 'seventies,
when leaded gasoline was on the way out,

but its sweet-smelling residue yet gilded asphalt.
A parking lot laps at the edges of my bad dreams, reservoir

from which the water drawn could quench
suffering but the taste would stop you cold,

like living in a museum, beneath
tall sealed windows and Corinthian shadows:

to never think of anything else but this one grief,
tar stele, oil swirled in bas relief.

Parking lots gather toxins: lead, mercury, toluene,
what ever they've added to gasoline to kill the knock.

I was a child there, angelic.
Automobiles of errant mothers swerved where I stepped.

Doors and Ghosts

Doors are the ghosts of the house,
between the living and the earth
doors trespass. Their costly weight
grasps and releases.
Doors violate the room: frame
the place where space closes and it's done.

Close your eyes and the grass
will shimmer under filaments
of retreating rain. Rain draws a door
across the unmendable broken yards.

Doors like trees seem to protect, or harm,
it all depends on the body's vantage,
and how steady the hands.
My hands have not been steady —

and lately I grow terrified of entry,
of the power of rooms
to mark fields that are almost human,
in the freaks and glints of evening light.

The sky shapes a door
and what has been ruined must be put away,
but I am daunted by bad dreams,
the doors of rain opening, fragile
across late oak and hickory.

Doors haunt me — going out, going in —
the brass tacks of gravity.

CLAIRE MILLIKIN

Knob and Tube

In walls, knob and tube wires shift like rain —
a sparking and deciduous line
that my grandfather followed, electrician.

Rain moves through the trees like wires,
its lines do not bring light
but something deeper,
sleep in a derelict house.

Rain's clean wires cleave to branches, worn brick.
The abandoned house cannot be salvaged —
I understand the limits
but a woman kneels in the grass.

Rain is ocean that has lost its way
and without redemption slips
into the fields, effigy, heart of Jesus.

I know there's no redemption
but, look, a woman kneels in the grass.

Eastern Seaboard
Greyhound Incantation

-- for Carol Bachofner

Ride up and down the eastern seaboard until it doesn't matter anymore
if the factories slip onto your fingers their shadow rings,
a desolate marriage: this is your country, the country of between. Ride
Georgia to Maine. The mirror night shapes against windows

shows a familiar face: curve that also was your mother's, cheekbones, eyes.
Sometimes take an apple for safekeeping against hunger.
Sometimes carry hunger. On Greyhound
you can shoulder the distance from your father's house,

where you will never be safe. And the boats of last century are mostly gone,
the taste of the bus bromide and vinyl, a toxic world above this world,
wheels circling delicate iridescent fires, transmuted spheres.

There's a space after dusk when you rake your fingers
and cannot dream without rehearsing the way your father pulled
back your face and milky late afternoon light tightened.

Lyres for the requiem fields farthest from highway, lyres of trees in spare rain,
basalt engine beginning and ending, ending and beginning: ride.

CLAIRE MILLIKIN

Toil of Birds

The grass was made for Sundays
where I grew up, in the folding shadow
of a blue-print house.

Blue paper walls caused unappeasable thirst.
Watching, I swallowed
nineteenth-century aesthetics,
azoth, dealbate, cinnabar, yellow tin:
pigments that paint the beautiful, irreversible damage within.

The grass kneels in wind,
woods are not always places of the dead
only sometimes between pines, listen.

This thread of homelessness cannot be raked from grass, or doorways, or
branches,
its laces fall between
the birds' late shifts
their cries, enigmatic, intent,
just beyond the unkept house.

Stray

At the end of childhood I slept in my car
nights, after summer had finished.
The car became my form:
anyone could see where I'd been,
cribbing the last of mother's inheritance.

Mother was a professional singer,
I slept outside the door of her voice
drenched evenings, when rain's
after-image pulled between branches
at the parking lot's edge.
At dusk there's nothing but distance
and the memory of your mother' voice, hitting the notes.

Turn the radio, she sings still, soft and full
at the edge of night where thin stars touch.

Divot in the grass where a doe kept,
last night, night before last: her form.

Baby blue sky between branches of pale oak,
of winter's pelage, this song to shadow sleep.

Insects

Past the last houses,
insects stitch back the woods,
a glistening
diminuendo at doorways,
trespass lintels, sills.

The ocean swallows all things, at last it will
rise, eustasy,
covering operas and cities, subways and desire, and the beautiful

hard equations: where the land ends,
insects lifting
on fragile, tensile wings into light.

Dynes

At age sixteen, I ran two hours without stopping
down the shore and back again.

We had just finished eating lunch and my father's student,
with whom he was sleeping, told a story
about being raped
on the subway, turning her face.

I trained distance in those days,
but running two hours without stopping was far even for me.

At noon I began running, the dunes
by my side shaped hallways, ocean waves
serrating the lines.

My shadow moved with me like bad nerves,
along the shore, mile into mile,
molt of sunlight that hurts
only afterwards, no bridges just jutting piers
to break the inhuman littoral zone.

Sometimes, I think even now of the small ungathered light
in tender stir of shallow ocean water at the edge.

Running mile by mile, my shadow became a fascicle,
leaf, paper, skin:
keep moving, along dunes a silhouette
swallowed by water tipping back
and forth, into and through itself.

Solitary Confinement

For two-and-a-half months I lived

in a locked room where light entered by slant of one

eastern window, watched

in the steel mirror sky

reflecting the edge of raw earth, tobacco fields' spilled rinds, inverted leaves

nicotinic bream, aciculate pines.

The meaning of it almost slips, but rises back

when yet again I have to eat

by remembering with the clarity of photographs.

They brought me food I refused, mostly, cusp of adolescence —

at fifteen years old I had left my mother's house and arrived through a forest

into juvenile corrections, paper house of the dispossessed.

There, my name grew thin:

I began to forget I had inherited the name of her mother

and of her mother. My hands slipped blue at dusks, almost starving

drawing again the line of pith, essential substance

the birds shadowed in a steel mirror

casting back what I knew

to say to pass through.

Swimming Pools of Western Georgia

The place that could drown you
can always return, like evening that settles
into leaves, imperceptible at first,

then wholly, and of absolute consequence, night.
A detent, a catch, that water of childhood
in which you learned to swim could still rise
and undo you, Tifton,

Georgia, rooms of milky light where the old women knelt
at the piano's itinerary of nostalgia
out of tune beneath photographs
of toothless ancestors.

It rises in you yet
the taste of that water, don't think it won't come back
to drown as you drowned before, immersion baptism,
cotton fields sprayed brilliant with pesticides.

For the sojourn can only last so long. You will have to swim again
as he first made you swim. Narrow shoulders exposed
you rose from the water, refused a towel,
the ropes of water sliding down
like Houdini.

Coming Home in Another Country

Undressing with my sisters
in the basement before the mirror,
stripping so we saw each other
naked as before marriage,
as mother once had dreamed us, snow
stapled the windows. Snow and late
afternoon rode the bus across the boundary.

Impossible to return
unchanged, snow shadows down dark shelves.
In the emptied room before the wedding,
a mirror coruscating
when trees glinted with ice. Let
snow open the raw fields
after harvest's torn symmetries.

My face has already been coined,
traded away,
at the way stations where men wait,
world after world.

The Sacrifice

Every day this month the grass tightens and heat lightning
scars the back of sky above fields.
Such was the kingdom of heaven
the summer she was killed,
for memory
is a fever returning through low waters.
In childhood's sideboard mirror our faces showed close.

But when the girl knelt
no one else watched,
just her father, his gun.

Her truckled shoulders slender in the way of young children,
red checked dress.
In aftermath, her mother opened windows, doors
and birds flew in, foxes stepped.
The aunts swept
the floor with their hands.

The Track's Late Mirrors

One afternoon when I was five years old
my father promised "if you run a mile
fast enough, I'll buy you ice cream from the store."
Light fell like cream along my ankles, gold buckles
of church shoes just after church.

In my yellow Sunday dress, I kept pace
with the clock he called into sky,
running hard, raveling breath
until I could see through
to the saints, the late mirrors,

my Mary Jane patent leathers
gleaming like spilled coins,
each strike of stride against tar,
planchets, blanks traded for no currency.

It hurts to go down that far, where oxygen ebbs.
Someone has to hold you down
face to the rough surface. Run fast enough:
every race I won afterwards
I remembered.

Vodka and Rice

I refused to eat the fish he caught,
each night getting drunker
stanching my stomach with white rice
until the world began to shake, whitely,
glittering like small polished grains,
shining like glass, and everything tasted of him
and vodka, and white rice.

White rice is another form of water —
monotonous whiteness took over, as if I were a bride,
in the gray room sodden by ocean,
a kind of desperate fall when you hear the waves,
like those paintings of Jesus on the cross,
for there's nothing to be done about it, after all.

A girl in a room in the corner of the house,
cigarette ashes and salt.
I was there only for him to enter,
but I kept a book and read it, lips, eyes

swirling with vodka, memorizing
the passages of words as if nothing
but words might soothe the world again,
and what vodka ruins, rice heals.

CLAIRE MILLIKIN

Duplicity

The fisherman with a hook in place of one hand
crossed before me, entering.
A damaged threshold,
that frame of peeling paint.

I loved the beauty of it, the metal hook,
an exact mark curved in sunlight.
The first day of thaw and snow
beginning to slip its folds,
audibly unfastening
above the door.

The hook was clean and hid nothing
like a poem replacing a hand.

That girl in Grimm's fairy-tale whose father
cut off her hands,
wasn't she cleaner, after,
her tears a refining fire?

She walked into the woods,
her hands strapped to her back.

In the same way, as a girl, I carried school books.
My mother was sure it was my fault,
that the books weight bent
my spine into this curve, that my body
drew my father's touch.

My words were cut off, strapped to my back.
Dry leaves hissed. I walked into the forest.

Virgin, Meditations

Into the almost empty room vines
of falling snow lineate
the cold. The small child goes and gets
the miniature of the Virgin,
icon set in gilt,
and hands it to me
without speaking.

Each letter could be the letter
from home wearing the news of his death,
like dreaming in that language
learned first, the one I swear
I've forgotten. The vines of snow

narrow. A colder weather
approaches the house. Snow
slips the lilacs' gaps, vineyard
wrested from rooms left clean:
the snow a house emptying itself.

As if I had never stood
naked, in a cold room,
holding against my body clothes
and screaming to my mother
to keep my father out.
My whole life marks
snow where the snow is stone,
a stela, a steep door.

CLAIRE MILLIKIN

Dining Hall Workers,
Yale University, circa 1990

There was no balm for AIDS then, no medicine
that worked. I drank my coffee from Styrofoam
that never disintegrates, lipstick swirled in the mix,
all summer, the eastern ocean shifting its white doors.

We moved between the colleges by steam tunnel, hypogeal,
forsaking sky and gardens. Student workers,

in the dining hall we served summer's customers, conferences of scientists
who winked at us both for we were of that same country,
deep South, pretty children, a girl, and a boy.

His hands shook, ladling potatoes, measuring exact and clean,
while I took the job carelessly, profligate
of men, unloved by my sisters who'd stayed home.
He and I stood side by side serving meat and apples
while summer moved beyond the dining hall, tensed brilliant, peripheral.

Each morning we opened the dining hall before first light, shared
cigarettes for their half-life, weight

for weight, cigarettes move easier than flesh —
quiddity substance they consume themselves —
the sickness had scarcely touched his skin.

All summer we served sustenance to others, viaticum,
the boy telling me how he was once the star

of the Baptist church choir, down home, a boy tenor of such purity,
immaculate voice.

Poppies

They breathe without skin,
messengers
pulsing at the Atlantic's edge.

Towards them, the waves move like postcards
white and blank, sent over and over.

Their red line is nothing
but an offering.
The woman who tends
the poppies
kneels. She is very old. Slowly,

over years, I have become part of her
world. I have gotten there
without talking,
returning
to this place near water.

The waves
forget the land—as soon as they turn
they have already forgotten.

I want to forget the well
in my body that cannot go dry,
the night whitening over
a square of sky. Then gulls,

with their cries
of pearl, carry it off.

Across the littorus, the cloth
of water, tears
and mends. Shadow,
the sister of water,

guards the poppies:
the heart,
the shining, sugary seeds.

CLAIRE MILLIKIN

Sweet Tooth

I used to fall asleep in my shoes,
the violence of sugar on my lips,
married to a jazz drummer in Texas,
almost every night a gig.

The desert matches what you lose,
step for step, its arid hasps
open the cinder block house of childhood's marriage
to swallow sugar instead of water, instead of meat, sugar

while the remex feathers of the Colorado river shift.
In the fall the river would almost disappear

but sugar cannot transevaporate,
it works inwards, along an inland tributary,
this place he touched
under the steps of frayed light, each time he went deeper

until I could not turn back
the hotel rooms dirty with silt,
beds tasting of weather.

Years later the tooth began to hurt,
the desert's snatches emptying my voice.
Trading on my compliance
he'd remove the shoes, laces frayed, ferrule
between his fingers.

We kept a kitchen of sugar,
so much sugar that we had to spray

for bugs until the air tasted always of chemical ruin, pesticides —

inland, under the boundaries,
whippoorwills lengthened their threading cries.

House in Closet

I built a house at the end of childhood
in the bedroom closet of a house we rented:
a house of shoe-boxes, wrapping paper, detritus,

wrapped the shoe-boxes in bright paper and foil
and fashioned furniture from pencils, flaking paint, metal wires;.
Working slowly, for in those days I was starving, stripping
my body of flesh like a penitent,

it wasn't clear what I regretted.
But as I grew less beautiful, shoulders sharpening
scalene, I looked nothing like a woman
and that made me happy.

The house in the closet grew finer, shining with trash resurrected,
paper salvaged from Christmas
and coins stolen from my father's bedside table
shaping low creches for invisible dolls.

Everything in those days had to be stolen,
or invisible:
the way a room closes sky inside.

In the closet I built
dioramas for dolls without dolls,
for months I worked. Then, the scenes complete

I'd crouch like an animal before a fire and stare for hours.
Antimere, between
trash and deity
my darkroom of inheritance.

Translator

As a child, I was a natural linguist.
Of necessity, I caught on to languages,
country to country, like counting
to your room by hotel hall doors.

We traveled between lexicons,
my small body in trains
shook and slept,
waking to each new station.

I watched the signs shift
at borders, and bartered
my words when we entered.
Our rented room stayed the same —

all rented rooms are one,
cradling what passes on —
a wash-stand, and mother's neck curved
to the water at evening,

her hair down, a dark swan.
She'd fit my whole body in the basin,
baptism before sleep, absolution.
Mornings, I had to forget

one language to climb
the ladder of the next.
Vocabularies entered me like breath.
But I have forgotten now

all those early tongues,
the way my father's hands
drew heavy curtains
and nothing more could be seen.

I speak without accent —
no language tags me.
Even this poem
washes clean.

Red Paint Fence

My father had us paint his fence.
I was two, my sister five.
Red primer, lead oxide,
an ancient can
pulled from the shed out back.

The fence squared
the yard's pool of grass,
honeysuckle, pine
and hickory leaning in. Gave us the paint
and, paying no attention, he walked off.

As siblings do, we fought.
High summer in the deep South, nearly
without clothes,
we coated each other's
naked arms and legs,
brushes dripping with the thick red stuff.

While no one watched
we attacked, furiously at first,
then tenderly,
attending to the job,
our small bodies at last utterly covered,

like Celts dyed in woad,
readied for battle,
or heroes in the tomb
laid in red ochre.

When mother found us
red evening was coming on
with its wall of shadows.
She said nothing, led us inside

to a turpentine bath.
I can still taste the bitter ring
of that water, stain
of my father, pressing into sleep.

CLAIRE MILLIKIN

Winter's Keys

Last night cold came back, like a leveling hand.
I went back by winter's ulterior map:
where we walked that hill outside Pittsboro, North Carolina
with my coat red-lined, for guilt,
and we spoke into a silencing wind.

Blown dirt leaned against us
as we moved in the dry grass.
Dusk tunneled the fields,
the light leaned sharp
making the field intimate and distant.
We came to the interior house.

This morning, shadows
marble the apartment's swept floors.
Winter rains freeze the alley trees.
Now, always, this empty place has been waiting.

Moving Out

Who can say
what turn of sky
makes the cold
a mirror.

We watch ourselves vanish
from this house.
Leaving in winter
I cannot stop

looking at my wrist.
The snow's white clock
shakes the hemlocks.
For safety pack the mirrors

in layers of soft cloth.
Spruce trees bell
against the panes.
The snow, moving rapidly, seems to hear.

In evergreens
each needle's vein
fastens into water,
carrying water from the under-earth's

unseen well, water that holds
out, that lasts.
Boxes build
new rooms within

the corners of our now emptied rooms,
or no longer ours,
who can say
what turn of sky.

CLAIRE MILLIKIN

Insomnia's Plow

Snow sounds its soft engine
interrupting grass and night.

 It sows its thousand-on-thousand seeds, each
grain with its own blankness,

what it buries, what it brings.
I hear the plow cross

dragging salt. Almost instantly
the street shuts back,

whiteness without furrow.
The doors of the snow open and close,

a series of doors to emptied rooms,
where my body works

like a mirror for my father
and the quicker I pull away

the harder he shuts the door.
Snow sinks the branches

of the orchard next-door.
The owners live beside it still,

 three ancient brothers. They watch
but no longer touch

to salvage, mend, or harvest.
I've also let things go—

 disinherited—
to breathe by this cold glass, watching

snow rise and drop, more and less
than breath's chilled arcs, the contrapuntal losses.

Skirting Homelessness

Wolf at the door, I have fed you, so many years —
my fingers sugar-tipped,
palms honey-dipped, my wrists jerking away
at the last slim chance,
your snout against my pulse.
Your fur's kept sleek with my losses.
I feed you the music of each dropped coin.

Once, on a train, I woke to a stranger
tracing his hands along my face — your underling,
I don't doubt it.
The sky drew cold at open windows
as we crossed into another country.

 I've appeased your maw with junked wedding rings,
and the names of boys who did not become husbands,
and cities of abandoned apartments, jobs
left precipitously, for nothing next.

Your hunger is tantamount
to my willingness. I tend you, as women dressed in black
mourning bring honeyed wheat and almonds,
kòliva, for the dead. Like them I kneel
and set down sweet food onto dirt.

For a time, you permitted me a house
near the ocean, where the coast's massive stones
satisfied your taste — and with you I drank
from a well red with iron.

By fields streaked with hematite, ringed
with sumac branches splitting into cries,
you offered me a child, and vanished.

 But now you're back, thinner than ever.
My hands reach out, no less tender.
Here are the keys to the car:
we drive everywhere, nowhere.

CLAIRE MILLIKIN

Car of Sky, Car of Earth

Mother's other sister drove a car with the floor
rusted out. Like her, the car had once been a beauty.

Gilded dented fenders glittered yet
when I rode beside her, a child. We never talked

for through the hole in the floor I watched
entranced as earth beneath the car move like water, ligure,

a treasure of gravel, asphalt gleaming through the town.
She let her teeth rot out and sought no doctor

for that fatal cough, cigarette by cigarette, mourning the small daughter
whom her husband had shot. I never asked

when I rode with her, for the car's open floor swept
too thrilling a vista — why ask —

unmask falling grass, lacquered stones, vermilion ravine.
Who in blood is saved,

who survives.
Rust dismantles, relict lines.

I used to beg to ride beside her, near twin of my mother,
her hands like oak leaves when winter's lambent harms

have slipped, iridescent, of sky as of earth.
To the damaged place I trained my gaze

through the gap. Lead gas fumes
sweetly burned. She drove

with skill unparalleled by any man yet,
though I have long practiced the passenger's craft.

The Terror of Objects

In those days I knew too much
about objects: not any particular object

but every thing, all
that had mass and form and weight, shape and heft

burned into my mind, and I knew them.
I could not stop watching and noticing each slant of wall, cleft of door,

the shoes worn by men and women, writing paraphernalia, cars.
The way some think only of sex, the rigging of desire,

I could not stop noticing the danger of objects — chairs, tables, lamps, mirrors
even cups bore weight that could harm, and gravity unpredictable,

gravity has never been proven, only intimated, repeated,
each object shining eerie.

I could not remember the world before violence
when doors worked like water,

iridescent surfaces, ghostlier flint of winter.
I could not forget that even holy books can damage if thrown

and that everything can be thrown, the body breaks down,
accidents happen and you kneel and your mother smiles,

telling you sit still, he did nothing wrong, water
sliding through folding leaves,
tarnished, childish soul.

Before Seat Belts

No barriers to gravity or velocity,
no harness in those days.

The trees wore their flags of stuttered light, and we rode open and unwieldy
in cars fleet with sky, windows rolled down
like the vanishing walls in dreams.

For the law of seatbelts yet waited, like new rain,
penumbra at the vanishing horizon,
in those days when no one
memorized the names of daughters.

Leaded turned the engine, lead that by alchemy makes gold
only the pain of that translation gets nearly unbearable,
how it hurts to burn away the dross
and take a name for yourself.

Your hands first and then your eyes singe
and then you set the mark
with your teeth, knees, if must be.

In childhood, we wore no seatbelts, and no one noticed.
We'd have flown like angels if cars collided,
deft velocity in the badlands of passage.

Dairy Queen Redux

My elder sister rests
her head against the window glass
as baby sister dances
in the center of the table, the youngest of us,
her fat legs turning beneath a thin yellow dress.
A dropped coin and my small sister starts swirling;

grandfather empties from his pocket planchets, blanks.
He will feed us this template of dusk,
infant dance on Formica table top —
pale cream flecked with frantic gold —
her feet flat against the cold surface,
her hands tilting up,
an unspeakable question posed.

Beyond the window, the fields split in their sling of too much rain,
along the edge of dirt our shadows troughed through glass.
In almost translucent dress, turns on the table the child
mirrored in night's address.
Salome asked nothing for herself
believing yet in the balm of mother's milk.

CLAIRE MILLIKIN

The Gardeners

One summer I rented a room with two gardeners, leased
on the cheap. During the days I slept in the room's one bed,

and the gardeners returned at dark, while I waited below
on notched steps just before walking to work,

smoking and listening
to the gardeners having sex without talking.

They never spoke to each other that I heard. They touched
the way you'd reach into earth

you do not coax. Understand, I was not in love with the gardeners.
Their faces neither ugly nor beautiful, their hands

liminal with dirt, carrying the nous, the boundary
that waits beneath beauty,

from scars heavy use
their arms nicked by tools — rakes, shovels, axes, hoes,

their knees racked with constant kneeling, like penitents.
Like penitents they knelt in the room making the floor give.

It is a story too late to tell, the third shift
I worked washing dishes, scraping clean the plates,

a skin of hunger working inwards,
the leavings of men on my palms and wrists.

Salt

The burn beneath things, sodium, volatile lineage
salt presses toward the east
where it dries in barrens, and mother's maiden name goes scant, a dead end.
Draft of salt, eversion, the earth turns out its wares.

A craving for salt goes with exile, the two cohere,
ghostly and peripatetic, in the parking lots of done marriages.
Sortilege, salt only heals by half.

Lay the table with salt, since some girls vanish.
The psalm of salt resists translation, branches of live oak
brunted. Salt burns beneath the level of seen things,
fugitive compound.

At the desks of young girls, salt should be used instead of ink, as antidote
against the way names get erased. At the table, an offering.
Daughters carry the line in secret, from the eastern flats
where sustenance dries into fragmentary lace.

Escutcheon, my fields were of salt,
and the vatic rhythm of salt filled my tongue,
a hinge of no name.

The Next Day

The day after my son was born
I lay him down on the bed beside me,
late afternoon. Late autumn

sun drew the room
out of itself, into the birches
and bare lilac branchings,
shading things obliquely,
as in photographs of departures
the shadows of hands.

I kept thinking to myself, this
is the first day of his life,
not the day he was born,
but the first real day, the aftermath.

After the three day birth,
he and I curled again alone
on the bed we'd inherited together.

I imagined I saw, almost, then
the last day of his life
as it would also come, next
century, when I would not be with him.
He was not really sleeping.
We watched each other carefully.

It was a beginning and an ending,
his life exchanged for something,
the way that trees at morning,
in any season, give away
for sun's astringent grains
the blurred divisions
that night permits, touch
without pressure, a shared pulse.

I barely touched him. Everything
had been broken apart. The drought
that autumn narrowing the wells,
my body unmade for his.

Filling Stations

The pumps look abandoned
but nothing can be abandoned completely —

lead gasoline seeps into the earth,
and the fountain drawn from ground water

tastes sweet with lead's flourish.
Gas stations, and not the church, shape the last lateral altars:

lean against cinderblock, derelict
angel, wearing your grandfather's coat.

He fought, a soldier,
but you're only a girl,

sheltering from fletchers of rain
at these narrow, penitential stations.

The boy who is pumping
might have been beautiful

if his face weren't pale with the weather of the underworld,
what's dredged up.

Still, you'd use what you buy here to go where you must.
Sacristy of outdated maps and aromatic burn,

when next door fields stir in icy air,
the way he moved through you. Walk

toward the vanishing point
into colder rain so your hands get clean.

TRANSIENTSHELTERS

Snow Rooms

i.
I want to speak like a child
as scant snow begins,
negligible little cuts at first,
paling between branches.

Listen, as an unfiltered wrest
of wind in dead vines
catches at some lesser cry, starts to rise
as dry fields marry a wet stain.

In the small rooms of our obeisance
there will only be snow to eat:
a wakeful substance,
it does not let us forget.

ii.
In an apartment above a river,
its curve stretching like bad sleep,
we lay out plates of cerulean,

cinnabar, vermilion, a cache of poisons
set clockwise round the table
towards the snow's dispersive sun.

Take up snow in bites and scraps
culled off the river's sweep
by gulls with arrow beaks;

I will wake from hunger after:
the sun doesn't touch the river,
however far East it goes.

The Rain Motel

i.
After the bus stations of childhood, it offers shelter
of a sort. Nebulae stitched together.

Lay my shoes at the threshold and enter:
rain shapes the walls translucent when calm, opaque in storm.

The rain motel shifts, one cannot trust it
but only here will they accept the currency I carry.

Doits, dismes, planchets, coins stolen from mother's emptied shelves.
Pay what must be paid, but get inside —

by slype, transept, duck
into this place the clock cannot translate.

ii.
In the rain motel empty my pockets,
cash on the mantel, silt.

Now any nightmare will be washed clear
I have only to get used to the constant threat to breath.

Deeper, into the lungs
rain sinks. Put away sky,

such delicacy
I once thought essential.

iii.
For those years I ate only candy, living off the hard stuff,
Life-savers, lollipops.
All the brain needs is sugar, nothing else.

Candy's small pulse divvied out my ascesis,
and the violence of sugar pulled my voice.

CLAIRE MILLIKIN

iv.
Years later, I still found evidence, warped
candies in the bottoms of discarded purses,
tinselly gold. I had only to love him,
evenings when it rained, the ruined material of need.

v.
Ramshackle motel, blue plateau
built of chit on chit of rain. The key

is to keep silent about how near
you live to homelessness. Tell no one

as you keep slipping deeper
into the motel's galactic whorl.

Coins

Don't tell the story, just trade the coins:
in the room that once was an attic with a mattress,
spilled change
an earlier tenant left.

I could not spend his money,
all from other countries,
but gathered the coins as tender
like Easter candy years after childhood.
On the chipped sill set my maquillage, in eggshell bottles.

The coins glinted miraculous:
from Cuba, Suriname, Luxembourg, Iceland.
All summer after my shift washing dishes
I let them open my fists,
which boys walked me back.
I could not trace myself any other way,

fingering the coins to palms.
The earlier tenant had also left behind
a pair of shoes and socks, clean, folded inside.

In echo I kept my dresses pressed, elegiac, immaculate.
I wanted nothing of the sun, summer's
coin impressed,
tracing my face — seal of eyes and lips.

Seven dresses in the closet of my extremity:
shoes I borrowed from the former tenant.

I paid my rent
in such currency,
sucking on coins to steel the wounds.

CLAIRE MILLIKIN

The Grift Apartment

At last, I had to rent the milk
from a woman deeper in the town, whose infant
had not been born alive.

She had it to give.
And I knew it would never work
any other way: his mouth on my skin
like the place in a bad dream
where you cannot say stop.

Milk from another woman, the lines of autumn
tightened through alleys and I could not let-down,
stuttering in that old language
I learned before I knew my name.

Stairs led upward toward a door with someone else's name
rubbed out. A third
apartment, without translation. The highway drew beyond
his infant voice, in the back room
where no windows caught truck fumes.

Late autumn turned inland,
following the canals, the brunt of ocean
with its briny milk of loss.

She fed him those first months,
an early snow tagging our hearts.

Returning from the Outer Banks, 1979

Just beyond the bridge, the child slid
from the truck stalled in traffic,
shaking her dark hair,
walked to get lemonade sold at the roadside, shoulders
burned beneath her thin halter.

She carried back to me, her best friend,
such sweetness, sugar
and lemon, a balance precarious
such fragile crossings:

take the wheel, seek an interim language
to speak

of the way they found her ten years later in that city —
not eating, unable to comprehend food, folded,

like estuary, half fresh, half salt,
as we drank tarnished water
with our fathers
before we were women.

One of two ways to tell a story, the same asylum
where she wound up.

Traffic narrows on bridges above ocean, psaltic
shadow-leaves
weave back and forth
above, along the waves.

CLAIRE MILLIKIN

Pure Substance

Since I could not feed him enough —
when autumn grew dry at orchards —
I taught the child haiku,
our words shimmering with hunger,
eastern hinge of sky a red coat.

I shrugged into my soldier grandfather's cast-off garment,
mannequin in the snow,
my shoulders fitting his when he fought for this country,
a slender boy.

Sugar augurs,
by bad teeth they will know the secret.

The child I could not feed
except with words
learned easily the practice of haiku,
his voice fluent and true,
the highway rattling its three lanes through
as he mastered the discipline.

Traces of grandfather's outlined wounds still showed
faintly, faintly stained inside the coat.
An echo persists like rain, its elemental sinking
in every word
if you chose right.

Milk teeth, each morning before first light
I'd put on grandfather's jacket,
walk to the store for bread and paper.

What survives: postcards, vanishing points,
Florentine art. At evening,

another woman's child crying through an open door.
Oneiric, the birds slipped upward into branches
in winter's red dusks.

The Animals of Rain

Their vagrant bodies ache to be clearly seen,
to materialize wholly, beyond shimmering.
Apodictic, they exist.
Only try to make them out:
the animals of rain mark their paces.

I have given myself away
my hands on the floor in recursive light.
Between the porches, the pale animals stalk, coffle.

The rain animals mean no harm
but crossing one could prove fatal
for they will kiss your hand as the faithful in church kiss the priest's
and then your thirst will never ease.

The rain animals sleep between frames
of window and door, their sleek forms
answer and disperse.

They covet milk and the dilapidated leaves of the honeysuckle.
I should never have come back to this place, never
have let him press me against the wall.

Give away what my open hands let slip.
It's not the fault of the animals
that I've lived in rental after rental, such ghosts
as correlate with used car dealers.

But the pleasures of rain persist. If you catch a rain animal,
lay your hands on the creature's pelt
your fingers damp
down its ineffable spine —

and the windows of your soul will shimmer
as if waking from winter torpor.

Marine

If you work here I will feed you, she promised
measuring my wrists, fragile,
in her palms and fingers.

So I took the job clearing tables
to follow a taste of her green eyes as she watched,
my arms quickly growing strong.

Emigrated here to get married,
but when we met she wept, *What have they done to you.*
She managed the late shift.

Clearing the last tables
I meticulously gathered
each transient relic,
uneaten food, snuffed cigarettes.

Its salt for your salt, pulse for pulse,
the ocean by America gets violent.

Outside, streets stuttered red with late
autumn, apples brilliant and shed—
how they tasted—sweetness at the verge of rot
chapeled on that low hill

across which moved the ocean
of night, paraphrastic
shadows shimmering through rooms,
for she hires you
into a future you cannot chose.

Autumn Taxi

In the spent fairgrounds light of late autumn
beside the rowed poplar trees,
a rickety taxi drives.
How many times have I ridden, following

campestral smoke from some unreachable house:
leaves ending their measure of sun, the animals and men
moving on to another town,
in intricate webs of rain.

I sought a bed
for the infant on the third story where she could watch the light shift,
for only the human world damages
a soul. Animals breaking
open the fields, swallowing time,

make no real difference.
The wind sounds like someone walking behind you,
past the places around roots
where the apple pickers snuffed cigarettes,
and a few windfall, ruby apples yet rest.

CLAIRE MILLIKIN

Jelly Fish

i.
When nothing's left but to enter the house
have mercy, for the jelly fish
takes no proxy, its mere touch can maim,
its sting nearly fatal;
on the inside of a young girl's thighs,
some wound in vision, amalgam
in blue hallways—
jump over the jelly-fish, do not brush
its flesh with even your smallest toe.

To once have been
the only animal in the ocean, to have outlasted
and find itself like a mirror stranded on sand, bested
by bony fish with eyes and sense— even the sharks anchor less
far back in history
than the jelly fish, its whole body atavistic, under tides.

ii.
How without bones or mind,
jelly fish takes back the ocean in rising heat, eustasy, primordial warmth,
that reminds me most of Tifton, Georgia.

The jellyfish keeps its secrets, no matter how transparent.
In warming oceans, it multiplies prodigiously. I've taken risks:
at evening the grass goes dark and, indoors, small lamps gleam,
terrain of golden damages,
behind doors, the undertow.

iii.
What stands exterior to its folds:
in the blue parallel
hallways of father's father's house,
mirrors and photographs face themselves
sinking lower and deeper.

No other kiss but my father's
for this translucent mesh.

Fireflies

Their pulse always hurts a little,
as if a small wound opened and closed again and again.

When I was a child, the grown-ups celebrated fireflies' return
after years of DDT

though crop dusters just sprayed the fields with something else. We punctured
tops of Mason jars, chasing and trapping

and captured the lit things alive
keeping fireflies by the bedside

so that no bad man will visit, ephemeral tarnished nightlight
such guilt to awaken and see them dead

in glib dawn light, detritus
after brilliance. Yet I never walked away

for the flickering of fireflies pulls
like the ache in your teeth when lightning comes closer.

A kind of resurrection they returned
but not unharmed by what had been done

in flushed corners of the fields where they were killed by pesticides,
killed not only singly but as a principle of light

vanishing into trees, the deft last turns
before he will collect you into that house.

The fireflies' thousand ulterior nerves
mark places where the world is too tender to touch,
its desolate rented rooms.

CLAIRE MILLIKIN

Fireflies returned after DDT was banned
and the aunts and uncles reached out to touch the insects, to catch them
hysterical and justified as saints.

When you wake in the bed
for wayward juveniles,
a glimmering light in the hall—
fireflies pulse, you could almost be home.

Hunters

In this season, a hunter
will cross the narrow road
through spare woods edging ocean,
balancing a careful gun.

Maple and birch have given up
their leaves, like breath,
and thin snow melts where it falls
on the still unfrozen earth

and on the deer's taut coats, ice
snuffed by their warm pelts.
When two muted shots
shock the sky like church-bells

crows circle the treetops,
marking the place of the kill:
I could walk straight there
arrowed, like the snow as it falls.

That winter before his death,
a buck in your father's fields
rose from behind a curve of rock.
He thought the deer spoke

to him in his illness.
Close to me now, the hunters work,
while snow gathers, spirituous,
erasing as it catches earth.

CLAIRE MILLIKIN

Outer Banks

My father once purchased
for each of his three daughters
one square–foot each
of an Outer Banks dune —

souvenir deeds pitched to tourists,
one square–foot berth,
per dollar, of the eroding earth.
All these years, I've kept my claim.

What's become of it, I sometimes wonder,
my childhood plot?
Scant land my father bought
I never sold to anyone.

For generations, that coast
has been vanishing into ocean.
Maybe my too early property
rides in the moon's hull and dray.

I have drifted north, ungathered
from my father,
who gave me nothing
but this more opulent third.

Late tonight, the earth's shadow falls across
a full moon. Snow
below turns to lunar substance.
The moon erodes downwards. Crushed

and smoothed, snow drifts deeper
here than childhood's dunes.
The lunar eclipse is barely seen:
clouds stanch the moon's ghost rim.

But the snow holds what remains
of the moon, its quality
of elegy, of losing ground.

Helen Moυγoυ

i.
You are the unmentioned,
a breath caught between words,
set away from the living, who go on talking.
Arrayed for your bridal — a nineteenth-century photograph
stashed in the third-floor attic —

first sister of his grandmother
to cross over, the eldest
leaving Piraeus by the Mediterranean,
the sun blinding as flash-powder off that sea.

Did you travel through Marseille?
through Liverpool? routes of immigrants and exiles,
or, like that first Helen,
were you secreted through Egypt?

What other images of you float up, elsewhere, unnamed, unmapped?
Years ago, the family stopped
searching for your grave
in steel-belt factory towns, where your trace ran out.

The last missive: blind with childbed fever, breathing rough,
your infant son dying with you,
did the American midwife
understand the words you cried out?

ii.
In the exposure-time of early photographs,
one kept as still as stone, lest
the contours of a face,
the gesture of a hand, blur
forever, imperfectly preserved.

CLAIRE MILLIKIN

Against the finished outline of your face
the framed glass mirrors
my living face, a palimpsest, intact —
trace upon earlier trace.

The damp of the Atlantic, its intimate salts, silver
mercuric, enter and erode —
blue attic walls, halides
xenos of colder skies.

Moon-Bathing

Swimming pool parking lot, late at night,
we climbed over the gate, bikes propped
against the padlock, trespassed
and lay down on asphalt, winnowed
of clothing to moon-bathe. Moon-bathe

to heal the damages of sun,
the moon's opposite latches
can unfasten singe,
the big girls telling me how it's done —
arrows silver and fatal
trapped Acteon.

We laid in moonlight
our wrists tense,
to be drawn in silver halide
a quiver, like photographs unsnapped.

It wasn't for death, only painlessness, that I pressed myself
to the crevice between mattress and the gap
of wall, his body filling the light on Naxos.

Later that summer, he crashed his bike
and I wore his clothes
until he healed.
My interim life left its mark, as in mirrors
or moonlight eyes have no sex.

Unlike the sun, moonlight burns
nothing. But your hands remember the lock
you opened, figuring the numbers, the sudden
nocked arrow shot.

CLAIRE MILLIKIN

Icarus, Girl

How can we be sure he was a son?
Wouldn't a father first turn such devotion
to a daughter, yoking feathers,
softest down, weight of the swan?

I was a gymnast
and threw myself against sky
that grew wider, turning above the balance beam,
in poised precarious abyss.

During flips, sometimes I'd think about fragility
like a bad dream that opens
in the day-time mind, heautoscopic,

the light pellucid as if I could lift myself endlessly
higher and higher,
for the body is not made of ashes
but of more fragile pulse, smaller than a door.

Once, upside down above the balance beam,
I contemplated my hands and feet that touched
in fetal tuck,
knew the strangeness of flight
which then began to unravel, Icarus—

as I uncoiled, dove down,
smashing against the beam, breaking
every bone in my right hand, snapping the wrist.

How can it be that Icarus was a son?
Wax melted and the feathers fell all at once.
My father awaited my nakedness.

For I too was a gymnast and danced in the sky
where it only hurts
afterward: remembering the light
that suddenly turned to gravity.

The priest on the midnight train north

He was waiting when I got to the end of the line,
nearly a guest of homelessness, one step ahead
of its fragile skin.
He'd tell me about his wife

whom he'd left to get consecrated, but still returned
some nights to her in secret, dark night of the soul.
The train took hours
to make its way from Boston north.

Frail sugar of leaves, oak and maple turning early,
milked with snow,
leaves scattered under spent trains, the engine worn
down by that time of night
like a bad sleep that must happen
anyway: you must at last lie down, and set the child
on your chest, his small weight for mercy.

It hurt me to travel like that, always
under the cast of snow, its disparate magnetic spall
chipped for crumbling prayer.

Every night I felt I could not possibly travel further,
but the train moved north.
In the farthest north, he would preach. How unfit the design

of light along the priest's hands
as the train crossed before factories
that never stopped. Long after midnight
light spooled from those buildings barring fields.

Train Set

In the third floor bedroom of the narrow apartment
we set up toy train tracks that circled the entire floor

no space was left empty, just tracks and imagined water
for the girl who was turning six years old, train set, circling the room

its pulse like a heart, what in quietness moves you
what causes your bones to sequester light.

Light moved quietly on her hands
as she called the trains to circle in ceaseless turn.

Stuttered arrows of rain flinching and vanishing and returning
from beyond the fields and graveyard next door.

The courtyard of Fidelity, merge of stones and new sky.
It was the beginning of history

when we bought the train set for his natural daughter
who was never supposed to be seen

in that apartment, a secret measure, her name his sister's name.
The train circled in night through night

for what else carries a train
but night sky and a girl's hands

who won't be claimed. And yet she slept there
in the room beneath us, the apartment narrow and high, mostly stairs.

The new world waited and turned back
on stone angels in the graveyard just past the child's window.

How voices in the courtyard will sound like the sky crossing glass
if rain solidifies suddenly to snow and its turning mirrors draw.

So her thin wrists balanced the cars
pulling through without accidents their cargo of empty doors.

Only a street left bearing your name, afterward,
with houses worth less and less, foreclosed.

Kafka Got Fat

I trusted only cafés to hold intact my body,
the offices of breakage sealed by coffee,
running my hands along translations, a few books I carried
in coat pockets.

The town's cafés like the stairs in Kafka's nightmares
where he'd grow fat despite careful diet
because the body longs for what vanishes. Always safest at the limit, the list
of streets: Fidelity, Star Route.

The rain clock shifted along the trees,
by the gas station
a low pink house where we slept on a mattress
and the scent of gasoline permeated our hair, making us love each other more.

The ocean, nowhere near, seemed to tether the end of each street and
Kafka could no longer climb stairs. Kafka got fat: he sucked all the mar-
row of the sacrificial lamb,
and I've got nothing left but the dry terrain of cafés, carrying my books
untranslated, xeric.

Kafka, he swallowed too much of the inwards stuff,
a pink house as we matched our bodies to our bodies, cars pulling in to fill up
the emptiness within, station
of engines, rain plowing the low mountains
past the city's hinge.

September Meny

i.
Truant, he will take you to the restaurant
at the adjunct of the town,
derelict September leaves repeating themselves
without repair, hiss across grass, asphalt.

He takes your hands
into his hands. Listen,
cicadas cry and vanish, moving deeper through their own voices.

September's choices, from which the color has leached away.
Don't risk speaking
the names of the dead and of foliage
immaterial to girls who must subsist in the woods
from which he once gathered you
as your father was driving deeper into Georgia.
Don't speak
for he will only move deeper into you

and there is nothing for it in the aftermath
light of September that witnesses.

ii.
If I wanted to say what I am I would show you
only a picture of my son.

But September marks me, listen, the cicadas are done
and the restaurant at that corner of the town never leaves,
always almost ruined

re-circulated
like codes of rain burned burgundy leaves.

Under the codes of rain his hands empty
against my shoulder, ribs, thighs. For the girls who walk deeper
into the woods, their backpacks harnessed

at crossroads must take what they can get, any ticket
any way back
to the human world.

Truant

How the girls past September disappear,
backpacks of haulm;
too tender now, they will not attend school
but buy smokes,
passing through priests who want nothing but to listen.

Disarmed, girls give up on school
and tell no one. They line up for the school bus in front
of their mothers' windows.
And then walk behind the bus,
melting into branches as it pulls east

where snow will settle along tobacco,
a few discarded soccer balls,
too intimate to catch.

The girls open their backpacks
and ease the thirst that releases no one,
not really, not even at night,

for you also will come upon your aunt and uncle sleeping
in the back bedroom in the house they have never cleaned.
Eleison, requiem for the truant girls.

I could recite their names but it would only
get them in trouble.

In My Mother's Closet

Late summer afternoons, hearing insects dying
against dry grass, unfastening the hasp
I would open her closet and crawl in, still
small enough for such purposes.

Lignin of grass carried on shoes into the closet,
I reached for the string of the bare bulb light
yanking open vision so it hurt, to behold
dresses her mother sewed by hand,
stitching down Batik linens,
impossible to wash without ruining.

The impossibility of getting clean
gets coded into summer's ending,
predicting the mattress in his father's abandoned house.

Dry light of insects on grass, succus,
how their wings fold, I wanted to understand the furrow,
just as I waited to understand my mother's clothes
in small boxes half emptied,

quick shadows in fields at the end of summer. Insects,
that bruised light inside. Look up:

desolate high summer light
sways the room out of itself.
Catalogue every object,
your mother's elegant
clothes from another country, unreclaimed.

Cherry Grove

When older girls walked
where the beach turned rough,
you, with your bare, tanned legs
would follow.

The land narrowed, sustaining a hunger,
some salt flats at the end
of summer, tracking
the big girls' footsteps

over oyster shells, middens, stones,
you'd go the length to sand's ledge.
With every step strip a layer
off the dwindling spit of land,

until you're walking on divided realms,
childhood's edge
under the austere cathedral light
that burns where disappear summer,

childhood, and solid ground. At the littoral zone
waiting for supper, to be fed —
a boy eating, holding out his hand,
and you step to him

past older girls standing in the wild air.

CLAIRE MILLIKIN

Eating from the Garden

In summer, when mother disappeared,
father fed us from his garden in the backyard.
Of unwashed vegetables caked still in dirt
he'd cook a strange stew
tomatoes, rhubarb.
From our red yard, we swallowed grit like penitents,
no longer wearing shoes.

His joy turned palpable, to answer no woman.
He'd harvest and feed us nothing but garden
until our teeth grew polished from chewing earth.

Once, while he shopped in town
we found the McDonald's parking lot,
frescoed shadows between hickory and oak.

All summer, I tried to steer clear of my father,
whose love ran too thick,
but the garden with its clay
marks the place where you're so hungry
you'll eat anyway.

My sisters collected fallen ketchup packets in that parking lot,
but I kept only salt, to wean myself
of his plundered, chthonic soups.

I swept the yard carefully,
and sun took my measure
as doors from the house swayed apart.

We could hear from the far clearing his singing, triumphant.
Scion, swallowing salt, I hardened.
In autumn, she returned.

Taking the Bus to Buy Make Up

The token in your palm marks you, gleaming and unprotected,
on a Saturday morning, having left your parents
sleeping in the house,
their sleep like folded cloth.

The glassed entrance to the mall reflects
in multiples your face, Veronica
so veiled by reflection.
Pulled by an undertow, emerge
to pass out of childhood alone.

Standing wordless at the counter,
beyond the aisles where girls turn beautiful,
at twelve-years-old
buy make-up —

a sweat-cloth, sudarium,
from the drug store —
of the town's one
half-trashed shopping mall. Ride
the bus home, then, open
windows above damp earth.

Michelangelo's Motel

There's always a room for me
in this motel, where the pieta
he refused to finish
haunts my bad dreams,
between forests and shopping malls
in the scantlings of America.

Virgin
who holds the tarnished fields,
Michelangelo's second-to-last pieta,
her face eroded, like a child
never taught to speak.

In the motel of what's cast away, it goes cheap
that flawed marble — from Carrera, Melos —
islands under hard sun.

We are not out of harm's way, yet,
the image is not done.

The pieta he left undone
I return to it:
because grief comes back,

it comes back and you will ride in the car
with any man who'll take you there
to the place where it hurts
enough to say her name.

After the Florentine Pieta

I too have tried to leave it,
deposition,
gathering my good skirt:
sleep here, cradled in the arms of a faceless mother.

On motel balconies, late in winter,
men grill contraband meat at evening
and the shoppers in the mall next door hum
a broken, clandestine vespers,

veins of sunlight through dust after heavy rain,
past the highway that looks eternal
anchored to its vanishing point.

The risk of rejecting the stone as he did
for its impurity —
that your face also
vanishes in a motel bathroom mirror
and you pay with a credit card
pretending your name is your mother's.

Luggage in Snow

Luggage is a kind of snow
and I will never get home carrying these garments
of winter folded
along with the suitcase of arrowheads
grandfather hoarded from childhood.

Language in snow takes one's pulse,
following the river, the railroad tracks:
I will never get home wearing snow on my back
its purlieu weft,
from harrowed fields.

I won't be a woman, just a carrier of snow.
Luggage and language hide desire:
remnants, fletchers.
And yet I cannot put it down, at evening walking
toward the rented room, its scarred chair.

Now pick up the telephone in the gap beneath stairs
there's no other voice but snow,
taking earth for stone.

The luggage grows heavier
so I will never reach her, now, my shoulders
remembering her shoulders

in the kitchen where she turned
formal leaves of ruby at evening, setting
knives in the drawer,
deft, delicate pace.

Patience

She telephones late at night,
her son taken by the county. In the doorway,
this eloquent dress
translucence cast by the car's headlights.

In profile her face held clear, but
Niobe wept endlessly
eroded by water and salt.

The direction of trees, just after rain, straightens
though wind blows sand
from the play-ground
into the church parking lot.

How shall I crouch beside it, now
how shall I dig in that pit in the side-yard,
where we dug as children,
hands in the dirt
to shape another fallen world?

CLAIRE MILLIKIN

Swimming Pool Keys

The year my cousin got killed, I learned to swim
stroking my small hands across the skin
of water in a pool in pinewoods where shadows stalled,
around my body, wholly formal.

I kept thinking she would come back,
reemerge in the place of shadows and water.

You can become homeless by degrees
or it can happen all at once.

After her husband killed their child, my aunt lost
the house, down from generations.

I once dreamed I searched for the keys to her house under water,
diving deeper to seek them submerged in that pool.

Each junket downward cost me, until I knew I would have to rise
and walk away empty
just to breathe.

In childhood, I already knew about the danger
of fathers, how long
to hold my tongue under water
the pool filling with earth and red needles.

Motel Limen

Of the paradigm of ocean,
but inland, the motel limen rises:
water shifts along the boundary
and you have nowhere else to sleep.

You can stay here as long as you want,
drinking from a bathroom sink
water that tastes brackish, drawn from beneath leaves, branches,
abandoned buildings,
beneath erosion
where the stones hold their mouths.

The motel takes on defunct marriages, and vanishing time. It
keeps company with dropped coins,
and your face in the mirror, curved by a scar.

How deep the touch went,
beneath foundations, rain sinking
to the roots of fields past the town.

Moths

— for Joan Braun

Narcotic, its element is salt without bitterness. Moth:
what gets set apart
from the fitful sleep of infants,
mothers walking them back and forth to rest —

to sleep now
without knowledge of having driven
all these years back and forth, obeisance
paid to the shuttered filling-stations

and abandoned roadside cafes
under snow's graphite, summoned lineage —
these scantly traveled back routes
of an itinerant kingdom.

Snow buries light into the road.
Its sift makes light tangible,
a risk for travel.
I'm crossing thresholds,

plural wings of moths
in fields rise and pulse, moths of snow
make the road shimmer, ineluctable
where I drive the curve.

My child, back in his crib, will not be touched,
but I open car windows to the vein, nervure
distilled from silver nitrate,
snow's interior.

The moth's stain, graph of scar
or ice, chimera-mirror,
here light the match
to snare the heart.

Milk

The dairy at the edge of town obsessed me.
I'd eaten nothing but fruit for months,
and the dairy advertised any kind of milk you wanted —
whole, cream, sugar-ice-churned,
fresh from cows pastured before plum orchards.

The herd fed off grass laden with drifting pesticides,
pesticides silted the shifting skies of my childhood.
At age fourteen, I sat on the bed of my gone aunt
and telephoned the dairy, asking for another sort of milk —
milk without calories, milk of transfiguration —

somehow to replenish my nearly wrecked flesh
and not gain an ounce. After the months of fasting
to shrive his touch, I wanted the opposite
of the laying on of hands, when the soul suddenly rises
through the body, sounded and damaged.

The woman who answered the dairy telephone did not understand —
for what I asked — milk of essence, without substance or heft,
milk of light, such as
I must once have drunk
from my mother before she gave me to my father,
and father's mother put me in
the front bedroom for daughters.

CLAIRE MILLIKIN

Gleaners

The gleaners will all gather snow, now,
the women in tobacco fields, their hands
shimmering as with strung pearl, curved
handful after handful
transient nacre, what transfigures, then goes.

Light slips
to a slow vestigial depth
in snowfall. Closing across the rays
of stubble, snow lacks roots. It hushes
into water's ceaseless, translucent
condensing down
into the tables of earth.

Past the fields' remnant task of harvest,
photographs and voices filter snow.
The way that nicotine enters blood
through skin, snow sinks
through us. The uninitiated
sicken, crouched,
sounding desire.

Abandoned by the sun
through porticoes, over stripped orchards,
at the limits, snow moves past any human door.
You tenderly light
a cigarette to pass across,
and the glaucous ashes glisten,
merge with snow.

Cocktail Parties

Autumn like a cocktail party shakes in the tired trees;
my small cousin and I got translated
like light between trees,
taken by grown-ups to parties.

The trees are losing
everything, gold and broken burgundy, tally
the way voices sound lost in houses,
pinewoods opening beyond the doorways.

No one knew
where it stood, the edge of pinewoods;
light shook in the wide and tall rooms
as if the houses were already partly forest.

Autumn like a cocktail party shakes in pines;
we'd wait in the corners, listening.
No one would check if we were hungry
but everyone loved us, enough to touch our hair.

Autumn touches the pale hickory leaves,
there's no other way through
summer's cost. My cousin and I knelt

in the back rooms of intricate houses;
at dusk we listened to them talk
the uncles, the fathers, a kind of fate in their voices.

Every house I only half inhabit
still listening for the half-light of autumn,
the cocktail hour
chiming just beyond the oak trees
clocks without mercy.

Salt Mosaic

There's no blood here, just a burgundy carpet
running the hall to the vanishing point.
On the stairs, a fan turns; grains of rice oxidize
in bowls of salt.

In the mirror in winter at the end of the hall,
my face almost
but not quite contained hers —

for the palace of salt has me, I am its best guest,
buying from its store trinkets of every sort —
vermeil rings and bracelets, necklaces of rain.
The coast leverages my fingers and ankles.

The museum guards could be gods
for my obeisance, they pay me little notice, but keep track
of the hours I give up
staring at salt's million fragments. Salt
lets nothing slip away,
even those months she was my daughter.

They fed us salt, summers, in childhood.
Salt preserves, lest loves evanesce, even this one.
Here are the ways to harvest salt: let the stuff evaporate
from beds along the sea,
or mine it
tugging the edges of sky and memory. Miscarry

another language to translate
the edge of sleep, speak
of the mirror at the end of the hall in winter,

a cold-snap
that never eases, down stairways, beyond doors,
translucent across earth.

Birds

The houses of other families: to enter them nights
for parties, like a bird through an open window.
I'd arrive, the temporary darling,
prettiest starling.

Furl of suspension
that coaxes birds above trees —
sometimes pulled me
as if my bones were hollow.

Birds, and the graphic shadows cast
by their flight, chart the town's limit
where the train line cedes to fields.
I will rent a thorough house,
slype of rain and torn leaves,
the last of mother's money paying my way.

It's no real property, just the worn
swallows singing,
not harshly,
but inhumanly clear.

Snow Chart

i.
A hunger remembered when hungry still
winter marks this ledger.
Snow-tallies, layers. In hard freeze,

nothing melts, gives through
to the under—world of wells, and shale, hypogeal
seeds, oil, ferric rivers
the ocean sieves down.

But oil, iron, earth, or salt
won't ease thirst.

On its body, the snow records its own
circlings and sinkings
the way a city answers by cross-streets
where you might have waited for him
at the corner of Prince and Mulberry.

A name, a husband, a church. Far and near now, snow
falls tintype into March. Hush,

snow descends and discards
into afterward.
There must be
nothing left to seed.

ii.
At the end of winter, a sostenuto
light extends cold hours, curve of fields.
Grave footprints to the doors,
still left from months ago.

It comes to itself and catches,
the empty, even rooms of snow
fat and blank as marrow,
the Virgin's skirts.

iii.
The snow marks its own departures.
One who cannot be reached.

Nearly exempt
from gravity, snow barely shifts. At all the windows
it begins again, carrying us farther in.

iv.
I calm myself by the child,
how he sleeps in the room,
sky curving through.

But nothing undoes the roads
where my father drives
night after night
in another country.

The train crosses
once each evening, behind
ice-breached orchards,
factories of frozen sand, the ocean
next door plying its stony wares.

v.
Hinged by heaped snow
on either side, the way
to the ocean narrows.

A tractor guides in its trailer hull a cull
of cracked bricks. A chimney once, a hearth
torn down. Late

afternoon sinks into deepening freeze. The road
comes to a house, then no house, only abandoned
ganister and lum, then ocean's
otherworldly hearth. The waves come
coupling sounds like open flames.

CLAIRE MILLIKIN

The Fisherman's Girls
on their Swing

Planted some two centuries back
these low orchards still bloom each year, first
flower the color of ash, then fruit:
apples, bitter and intact that no one harvests. Too small

for school, the fisherman's motherless girls
pump high on their swing of green-painted metal,
disappearing and re-appearing just above the roof,

rising from behind their low house, across
the alley from our house. As they swing, deep snow
folds the girls' shadows.

Their faces light clean
at the top of each curve,
then they sink, vanishing,
behind the house
flight, in its rapid masts.

Motherless, quicksilver
snow above the round nubs
of what will be fruit.

At evening, fields, voices, roads
narrow to one point:
the ocean's intimate
departures and returns, beneath
snow's mothering weight.

The Place

In the hotel at night my baby sister awakened me, weeping.

They had vanished into their thirst again, mother, father;
and we, age one and three,
caught in the room where they left us, in the old city.
I had not yet learned the name of that country.

But I'd already cadged some words
from its language, and crossed the hall
to knock on the door where a man in pajamas without a top
answered, delicately shielding my face from his crotch.

The baby is crying, I explained, facing his cigarette,
speaking his tongue, and he came across
to sit in the chair of the room and smoke
drag after drag watching the pale sky cross —
high summer in the far north, frayed curtains' palest gold.

I've never been able to translate the gold
back into my hands or lips, the sky itinerant and full
of that lost, earliest language, night
stemming the room where the baby slept again
because I had told her to sleep, *it's okay now,*

I told her to sleep
for I would stay awake and watch
while the man who could have done anything
smoked through pack after pack, telling me
a story, low and careful
in that language
that I have forgotten except when I awaken
answering bad dreams, and know the place again.

March Thaw by
the Abandoned House

The long freeze unlatches
in rain's opening hands.
Each slick shore road reaches
at the shore its own end.

We hear the forest next door, branch by branch
half deciduous, and at its edge
the abandoned house
taking in water like desire,
as water flows from ice.

All evening the children crouch
listening as rain gets faster.
A snow eating fog
comes on. I imagine how

it happens: to a house
only half emptied of belongings
the family, one by one, stop coming home,
leaving intact the pantry, the curtains
for deer and sky to fathom.

The First Apartment

The rooms smelled of sharp polished wood,
rich and tannic — equatorial afternoons,
quiet, a mother and her little daughters
waiting, on their own, like travelers for a train

without a schedule, a language
the mother had never learned to speak.
She never learned to speak in that country.
Curtains closed, in the long dark room

the mother would lie half-asleep, forgetful
of what breathed around her, her infant
awake, watching the intaglio of shadows.
Most afternoons, *amah* fed the small girl soup, salty and oily,

memorial food, viaticum, for infants and the ill,
for travelers, feverish, in the hinterlands.
She moved gently in that half light, that hard quiet,
like a soul learning early the quietness of death,

teaching the infant girl small morsels of her language.
Its clean, incised tones echoed and embalmed
the healing child, waiting out dusk malarial
afternoons of fever sleep and sweet resins,

while mother, closed eyes, folded her hands.
Always ready but unable to leave, exiles
expecting word they've been recalled,
looking out for a father's return, to be ferried

across two oceans, in time
for a new daughter to be born.

Hieratic

My parents' cocktail hour
rode the ridge between dark, resinous pines
like lights of an oncoming car
that mount a hill and cast a cool,
warning fire beyond the crest.

It's a car I always swerve from,
again and again, driving the ice
slicked roads home,
to another man emptily breathing.

This is his house and it is winter. Alcohol marks the air.
Sometimes father had me take a turn
carrying, shakily, drinks to the men.
Flanged dark pressed in
by stripped windows to the east.

I alone picked up the emptied glasses afterwards.
Not to speak
of what lightens at the window
as a car passes in the pith of night,

headlights' transient, hollow beams
warming nothing but burning
out at the rim of sleep, waking
to the skid I can't pull out of.

Temporal Residue

Go to sleep now, let closed eyes
erase the rain-luminous
farms surrounding, each getting sold
off acre by acre. To the body, time costs more:

watches once were painted with radium
radioactive dials and numbers,
luminescent, glowing blue like television
that cures and seals the soul, its lunar stain,
all primordial trace, flint echo.

The moon only reflects time
and cannot make it stop. In sleep,
a clock inherited will rein
your hands and mouth. A woman's bones

mistake radium for calcium,
bad milk
that empties synonyms of their translation, metic,
sojourner, vanishing into numbers.

Go to sleep: for only the numbers wait
fragile variants of long-ago shattered stars
like cars that skid
and cannot straighten.

Winter-Deaf

Cracked stint of last oak-leaves on branches — skidding vagrant
across thin ice — I can still hear those fine declensions,
but a deafness has begun
to open its ghostlier knowledge,
interior aural damage
inherited from my mother, and great-grandmother,
down the maternal line
from the first disappeared name.

From the boarded-up house's exhausted garden, scavenge.

Without leave
to borrow the land's prospect, trespassing with the wind
in my ears, it brings deafness
cast in icy oaks, low frozen pools,
flint and caress, inheritance
of what gets erased, the sounds that do not ease.

Farther down the mountain's curve
emerge young trees among stones
where a chimney once stood,
deserted lum.

A marriage I once drove towards,
the car hurtling north
to find this ruin
in his track-scarred arms.

End of Season

For the last time this season,
the girl wades out
to her father's lobster–boat.

Not yet thirteen,
she's already watched
my infant son, earning
a little candy money.

From shore, I watch the late, stripped
sky support itself
against her back,
her long, tied hair
thick as mooring rope,
dragging
as she walks
through windy, rising water,

the sunlight turning her older.
Must we always go
off with our fathers,
must they always come
to get us in their battered boats?

The bright green paint lobstermen use on hulls,
thick with mercury and lead
to withstand ocean's ravages,
glints mimetic with each wave's glance.

The last sign before the ocean
reads: Do not take the beach rocks.

My small son, assiduous,
sits gathering every rock he can.
Each smooth stone an obulus,
he hands them to me, the weight gathers
in my pocket. I live here, house–wife,
tending to winter.
Packed cars of tourists
   drive south.

My Mother's Car

When will my mother arrive, turning up at last,
driving her blue car by water, saving me
when I'm walking away
from the last of the houses gotten
by husbands, walking down the road
into the hushed substance of rain
that divides stones by breath,

past leaves not crushed but impressed against the road's edge
asphalt, gravel, stubble fields:
when will she show, driving her car
for which I have kept a look-out since I began
thirty years back, turning
my head for the game of rain, and desire,
its delicate, ephemeral marks.

There's no good time for suffering
but when she drives up in the blue car of thirst,
I will step in, without hesitating
and straighten my heart to the chassis.

I will tell her my teeth hurt and it's too late for milk. No matter
the rain knows the silk of which we are made,
down by the water, the red and gray boats.

When I am alone after the houses of men
she will arrive, then, as after gymnastics practice in childhood,
when I waited longest of all the girls,
shivering in tights and leotard,
and she furious as I opened the door —
What do you want of me, is there no one else

But the rain keeps only one car,
her hands sleek on the steering wheel, turning the key.

I've walked too far along the edge of things,
but she will get me, at last, with her map of erased names,
a family history submerged.

Downstairs there stir other worlds. But
this illness of childhood is incurable.
On the harbor's severe and horizontal star, rest the dark boats.

Soldier

After the war, we stayed in those motels,
in the parking lots, diesel trucks idling
all night. That's the way a diesel engine runs.

We got sustenance from vending,
for supper dry candy bars, packets of salt.
The road blurred into rain-slick mirrors.

I held my hands to the machine,
walked up the outdoor stairs into rain.
Underneath,
water and shadow share one pulse.

The beds where we slept
got borrowed by grown ups,
ilative, the adults
moved our small bodies to the floor.

In half sleep I still reach out my hands
not to fall.

Narthex

i.
Place your shoes on the backseat.
It will not rain or snow until you've found her,
furious for the wait.

Walk into the evening parking lot, carrying your en pointe shoes stitched
heavily at the toes,
no wings but the trees verge to shadows.

Suppertime for other girls, but we will walk into Fowler's
Food-store, and purchase the last derelict fruits
that he sells at evening,
sunk in his cups, his hands along the counter. It is our history

don't turn away, for the fine stillness afterward
lies worthy of your mother's country,
where you will not be fed

but offered a car filled with night sky.
Move through thin rain, toward no house.

ii.
For who will develop the image of dusk's parking lot,
carrying your ballet slippers, for protection

move past the one-hour photograph store, closed for the night,
your hands on the small pockets of your bones

exposed beneath leotard and tights,
and dance, back

where there are no photographs,
only your mother waiting with her long black hair
down past her hips,
vinyl seats shining and the dashboard swept.

Another Man's Coat

Your hands shaking like a secret cough
in the pockets of his cast-off coat,
walk by station walls diesel-cauled
like candle-blackened church interiors.

No one knows what your father did
but his family, and they do not care.
Buy that bread now, go purchase
with your mother's cash

the warm, soft, sweetness
from the baker who sells only to passengers.
The silence it will shape in your mouth
will let you enter the church

and pay a dollar
for a candle to light,
a prayer that touches the walls
of the sanctuary where, very late, you will arrive.

Fresh Paint

At all the gaps where the house had been stripped
to sell stood autumn —
hieratic lines of willow and oak.
We slept in my childhood bed,
beyond fields in western Georgia.

We slept together against the hard weather,
December house without heat, emptied for movers.
It reeked of fresh paint, a kind of violence,
we touched and moved into winter.

Knees, elbows, cheeks,
the willow trees had nothing to do with it —
erase even the oak leaves
to an open place inside, distal,
what vanishes.

We stayed just long enough
to end the house,
swallowing rice and milk
from swept cupboards.

Paint still has lead, the legal limit a low percentage,
for there is always a level of harm

that will be allowed,
a poison permitted in small doses.
In fields, snow moved like a clock — a prowess
at disappearing I learned then and never forgot.

Transatlantic Flights

— for Ellie

How will we sew back the cut
through which the airplane flies
almost evading gravity, amber light
slipping through clouds' grisaille.

It hurts to fly, to let the machine carry your body
through some limit you will never touch, but almost
as the mind is almost a machine, and yet
something's always left
in excess, longing.

Bring your camera, it will protect you, periapt
if they swerve too close to the nerve, nervure, the vein of light.

Some risk to balance there, brilliant against the window
tracing the land's limit,
until the doors twitch in grass.

In flight the food they offer, viaticum,
assuages such hunger for ascension: do not be afraid
when the plane bends, interstitial,
and rights itself, cloud turbulence only, not cumulous tumulus.

Our mothers could not keep us calm,
when we were infants in war zones.
Maybe that's the reason?

At the end of the nineteen-seventies, I could turn one hundred back flips
in a row on the backyard trampoline, not yet ten years old.
I weighed fifty pounds
and risked flight without a cry. How it tightens later,

gravity's hold, flex
that catches all and lets it fall.

Weaning

For a while after
there is still milk. Remnant
like the train station

in Durham, North Carolina
I always thought abandoned until
I left my parents from it

a platform redolent
with tobacco's sugar and ash scent,
weather of my childhood. The milk

doesn't just dry up. White drops
fall, vestigial
like tears on the faces

of carved, painted saints
in another country's
Medieval churches —

I visited once, a child —
kneeling confused
in Protestant reverence.

Like a censer, that nearly empty train
swung slowly past tobacco fields,
then picked up speed, crossing

out of the South. The Byzantine
icons I now keep
in a house up north

never smile or weep.
I have married into them.
Cold stoics, they fasten

CLAIRE MILLIKIN

the corner of the room
where I and my infant son
wait each other out, learning

to be abandoned and to abandon
in a season of late, pivotal snows.

Leaving the Hotel

Take with you the salvaged
spare change, worn running shoes, crushed baseball cap.
Anything left here will be lost for good.

Crouch on the floor by the defunct radiator
each coin paid you must steal back,
forcing the machine of your soul.

Take back every word
once spoken to persuade them to let you stay,
each man you stepped with, forget —
anything that slips here
sinks absolutely down, unfolded depth.

When you leave the room, shoulder the fragments
of liturgy from the chapel in the city.
Traffic shimmers,
the small gods of passage.

How you got to the hotel — don't try to remember,
only meditate the virtues, a few belongings —
baseball cap, coins, battered running shoes.

The hotel shakes with autumn's bad story
the one about leaves falling, ablative,
into vanishing light.

When you go, take every language
you can scrounge, because you'll have to read it straight
without translating, now,
the book of escape and survival,
all night, every night, for no television soul.

CLAIRE MILLIKIN

ACKNOWLEDGEMENTS

"Hand in Glove" appeared in *Cold Mountain Review*; "Hunters" appeared in *Off the Coast*; "Weaning" and "The Next Day "appeared in the anthology *White Ink: Poems on Mothers and Motherhood* (Demeter Press); "Outer Banks" appeared in the *North Carolina Literary Review*; "Snow Rooms" and "Dusk Waitress" appeared in alternate versions of *Motels Where We Lived* (Unicorn).

I also want to add here, heartfelt thanks to Gabrielle David for inspiration and wisdom. And thanks to Joan and Henry Braun for heir friendship and support through the years, as well as thanks to George V. Van DeVenter and the late Constance Hunting, who were so kind to me the years I was in Maine. In Virginia, Alison Booth and Lisa Russ Spaar have stood by me, and my gratitude to them is profound. Lastly, thanks to my husband Mark Raymond, who has done that difficult and mysterious thing of allowing poems to be written.

ABOUT THE POET

PHOTO: Elisabeth Hogeman

CLAIRE MILLIKIN grew up in Georgia, North Carolina, and overseas. She received her BA in Philosophy from Yale University; earned her MFA in poetry from New York University, and PhD in English Literature from the Graduate Center of the City University of New York. She currently teaches Art History and Sociology, as a Lecturer at University of Virginia.

Her poetry has appeared in numerous literary journals and magazines, including *Crab Orchid Review, Alabama Literary Review, North American Review, Iris: A Journal About Women, Willow Review, Ekphrasis, The Southern Poetry Review, Off the Coast, North Carolina Literary Review*, among others. Millikin has published the chapbook *The Gleaners* (Tiger's Eye Press, 2013), and her first poetry collection, *Museum of Snow* (Grayson Books, 2013).

Millikin participates in numerous conferences, colloquia, presentations and workshops around the country, that capture a wide range of topics, including women's literature, femininity, gender and violence, gothic and ghosts, poverty and race relations. Her fellowships, honors and awards include Excellence in Diversity Fellow (Univ. of Virginia, 2011-2012); The Carolyn G. Heilbrun Dissertation Prize (2003); and The Helene Newstead Dissertation Year Fellowship (Graduate Center, CUNY, 2000-2002). Visit her website at http://www.claireraymond.org. ❖

OTHER BOOKS BY 2LEAF PRESS

2LEAF PRESS challenges the status quo by publishing alternative fiction, non-fiction, poetry and bilingual works by activists, academics, poets and authors dedicated to diversity and social justice with scholarship that is accessible to the general public. 2LEAF PRESS produces high quality and beautifully produced hardcover, paperback and ebook formats through our series: *2LP Explorations in Diversity, 2LP University Books, 2LP Classics, 2LP Translations, Nuyorican World Series,* and *2LP Current Affairs, Culture & Politics.* Below is a selection of 2LEAF PRESS' published titles.

2LP EXPLORATIONS IN DIVERSITY

Substance of Fire: Gender and Race in the College Classroom
by Claire Millikin
Foreword by R. Joseph Rodríguez, Afterword by Richard Delgado
Contributed material by Riley Blanks, Blake Calhoun, Rox Trujillo

Black Lives Have Always Mattered
A Collection of Essays, Poems, and Personal Narratives
Edited by Abiodun Oyewole

The Beiging of America:
Personal Narratives about Being Mixed Race in the 21st Century
Edited by Cathy J. Schlund-Vials, Sean Frederick Forbes, Tara Betts
with an Afterword by Heidi Durrow

What Does it Mean to be White in America?
Breaking the White Code of Silence, A Collection of Personal Narratives
Edited by Gabrielle David and Sean Frederick Forbes
Introduction by Debby Irving and Afterword by Tara Betts

2LP UNIVERSITY BOOKS
Designs of Blackness, Mappings in the Literature and
Culture of African Americans
A. Robert Lee
20TH ANNIVERSARY EXPANDED EDITION

2LP CLASSICS
Adventures in Black and White
Edited and with a critical introduction by Tara Betts
by Philippa Duke Schuyler

Monsters: Mary Shelley's Frankenstein and Mathilda
by Mary Shelley, edited by Claire Millikin Raymond

2LP TRANSLATIONS
Birds on the Kiswar Tree
by Odi Gonzales, Translated by Lynn Levin
Bilingual: English/Spanish

Incessant Beauty, A Bilingual Anthology
by Ana Rossetti, Edited and Translated by Carmela Ferradáns
Bilingual: English/Spanish

NUYORICAN WORLD SERIES
Our Nuyorican Thing, The Birth of a Self-Made Identity
by Samuel Carrion Diaz, with an Introduction by Urayoán Noel
Bilingual: English/Spanish

Hey Yo! Yo Soy!, 40 Years of Nuyorican Street Poetry,
The Collected Works of Jesús Papoleto Meléndez
Bilingual: English/Spanish

LITERARY NONFICTION
No Vacancy; Homeless Women in Paradise
by Michael Reid

The Beauty of Being, A Collection of Fables, Short Stories & Essays
by Abiodun Oyewole

WHEREABOUTS: Stepping Out of Place,
An Outside in Literary & Travel Magazine Anthology
Edited by Brandi Dawn Henderson

PLAYS
Rivers of Women, The Play
by Shirley Bradley LeFlore, with photographs by Michael J. Bracey

AUTOBIOGRAPHIES/MEMOIRS/BIOGRAPHIES
Trailblazers, Black Women Who Helped Make America Great
American Firsts/American Icons
by Gabrielle David

Mother of Orphans
The True and Curious Story of Irish Alice, A Colored Man's Widow
by Dedria Humphries Barker

Strength of Soul
by Naomi Raquel Enright

Dream of the Water Children:
Memory and Mourning in the Black Pacific
by Fredrick D. Kakinami Cloyd
Foreword by Velina Hasu Houston, Introduction by Gerald Horne
Edited by Karen Chau

The Fourth Moment: Journeys from the Known to the Unknown, A Memoir
by Carole J. Garrison, Introduction by Sarah Willis

POETRY
PAPOLíTICO, Poems of a Political Persuasion
by Jesús Papoleto Meléndez
with an Introduction by Joel Kovel and DeeDee Halleck

Critics of Mystery Marvel, Collected Poems
by Youssef Alaoui, with an Introduction by Laila Halaby

shrimp
by jason vasser-elong, with an Introduction by Michael Castro
The Revlon Slough, New and Selected Poems
by Ray DiZazzo, with an Introduction by Claire Millikin

Written Eye: Visuals/Verse
by A. Robert Lee

A Country Without Borders: Poems and Stories of Kashmir
by Lalita Pandit Hogan, with an Introduction by Frederick Luis Aldama

Branches of the Tree of Life
The Collected Poems of Abiodun Oyewole 1969-2013
by Abiodun Oyewole, edited by Gabrielle David
with an Introduction by Betty J. Dopson

2Leaf Press is an imprint owned and operated by the Intercultural Alliance of Artists & Scholars, Inc. (IAAS), a NY-based nonprofit organization that publishes and promotes multicultural literature.

NEW YORK
www.2leafpress.org